A Soft Walk Through the Bible

Linda Sue Hand Hayes

Cover photo was taken by Chad McGlamery,
son of the author.

copyright © 2023 Linda Sue Hand Hayes
ISBN: 978-1-959700-07-4

Table of Contents

Dedications & Acknowledgments xxiii
Testimonials from Group Members xxiv
Chapter 1 1
   Lessons 1 and 2 1
      The Beginning, The Creation 1
      Adam 2
      The Garden of Eden 2
      Satan 3
      Serpent and Eve 3
      The Fall 3
   Lesson 3 3
      Adam and Eve and God 3
      God Speaking to the Serpent, Adam, and Eve 4
      Adam and Eve Sent From the Garden of Eden 5
      Cherubim 5
      Flaming Sword 5
      Children Born to Adam and Eve 5
      Cain and Able Give Offerings to God 6
      The First Murder 6
      God and Cain 6
      Cain Cursed 7
      God and Cain 7
      Genesis 4: 16-18 8
      Genesis 5: 28 -32 8
      Birth of Third Son, Seth 8
      Adam's Descendants 8
      Adam and Eve's Third Son, Seth 9
      Genesis 6: 1-4 9
      The Ungodly Line of Cain and the Godly Line of Seth 10

- Lesson Four 10
  - The Great Flood 10
  - Noah Builds The Ark 11
  - God's Promise to Noah- The Covenant 11
  - Orders From God 12
  - Animals Enter the Ark 12
  - Genesis 8 13
  - Noah's Ark Rests on the Mountain of Ararat 14
  - God Tells Noah to Leave the Ark 14
  - Genesis 8 14
  - God's Blessing 15
  - Noah and God's Covenant 15
  - The Rainbow 15
- Lesson 5 16
  - Job 1: 1-3 16
  - Job 1: 4-5 16
  - Satan Tempts Jesus 17
  - Afflictions of Job 17
  - Sabeans 18
  - Job 1: 16-19 18
  - Job Worships the LORD 18
  - Satan's Failure 19
  - Job's Second Affliction by Satan 19
  - Job 2: 7-8 20
  - Job's Wife Speaks 20
  - Three of Job's Friends Arrive 20
  - Job Cursed His Birth 21
  - Job Longs for Death 21
  - Tower of Babel 21

Chapter 2 22
- Lesson 1 22

- Genesis 9: 20-24 22
- Genesis 11:31-32 22
- Sarai 23
- Genesis 12: 1-4 23
- Abram Deceives the Egyptians 23
- Genesis12: 17-20 24
- Genesis 13: 1-4 24
- Abram and Lot Part Ways 24
- The Covenant Renewed by God 25
- Lot, Abram's Nephew 25
- Downfall of Sodom and Gomorrah 25
- Abraham Asks God to Spare Sodom 25
- Lot Sees Two Angels 26
- Evil Men Call Out to Lot 26
- Lot's Family Flees Sodom 27
- Destruction of Sodom and Gomorrah 27
- Lot's Daughters Have Sons 28
- Lesson 2 28
  - Abram and Sarai 28
  - Genesis 16 29
  - Hagar 29
  - Birth of Ishmael 29
  - Genesis 17: 18-22 30
  - Covenant Between God and Abram 30
  - From Abram to Abraham 30
  - God's Promise of a Son 31
  - Circumcision of Abraham's House 31
  - Three Visitors From Heaven 31
  - The Promise that Made Sarah Laugh to Herself 32
  - Isaac Born to Abraham and Sarah 32
  - Abraham's Son to Be a Sacrifice 32

- God Provides a Sacrifice for Abraham 33
- God Blesses Abraham 34
- Lesson 3 34
  - Rebekah, Esau, and Jacob 34
  - Sarah Dies and is Buried 34
  - Abraham Sends His Servant to Find a Wife for Isaac 35
  - The Servant Prays for Isaac's Wife 35
  - Rebekah 36
  - The Servant Tells Why He Came 37
  - Bethuel, Rebekah's Father, Says She Can Go 37
  - The Servant Said, "Let Us Go to My Master." 38
  - Rebekah Leaves 38
  - Rebekah Becomes Isaac's Wife 38
  - Abraham's Gifts to His Descendants 39
  - Abraham's Death and Burial 39
  - Rebekah Has Twins 39
  - Esau Bargains With Jacob 40
  - Isaac Wants to Bless Esau 40
  - The Plot Against Esau 41
  - Jacob Lies to His Father 41
  - Isaac Believes Jacob is Esau 42
  - Jacob Received the Blessing 42
  - Esau Weeps 42
  - Revenge Planned by Esau 43
  - No Wife from Canaan for Jacob 43
  - Ladder to Heaven 44
  - Jacob's Pledge to God 44
  - Jacob and Rachel 45
  - Jacob Works for Laban 45
  - Leah Has Children and Their Maidservant 46
  - Leah's First Four Sons 46

    Judah 47

    God Remembered Rachel and She Conceived 47

    Jacob Wants to Leave 47

    Jacob Listens to God 48

    Jacob Goes on His Way 48

    Jacob Asks God for Deliverance 49

    Jacob Sends Gifts to Esau 49

    Jacob and an Angel 50

Lesson 4 50

    Jacob's Name is Changed 50

    The Twins Meet Again 50

    Rachel Dies Giving Birth to Her Second Son 51

    Jacob's Sons 51

    Jacob and Esau Bury Their Father, Isaac 52

    The 12 Tribes of Israel 52

    Jacob Buys Land in Canaan 53

    Dinah, Jacob's Daughter Defiled 53

    Brothers to the Rescue 54

    The Brothers Get Revenge 54

Lesson 5 55

    Joseph's Coat of Many Colors 55

    Joseph's Dream 55

    Another Dream 55

    Israel Sends Joseph to Look for His Brothers 56

    The Plot to Get Rid of Joseph 56

    Joseph Sold for Twenty Pieces of Silver 57

    Brothers Lie to Jacob 57

    Joseph Heading to Egypt 57

    The Lord is With Joseph 58

    Joseph Refused the Master's Wife 58

    Wife Lies to Her Husband, Potiphar 58

Butler and Baker Offend Pharaoh	59
The Butler and Baker Have Dreams	59
Butler's Dream	59
"Remember Me," said Joseph.	60
Baker's Dream	60
The Dreams Become Reality	60
Pharaoh's Dreams	61
The Butler Remembers Joseph	61
Pharaoh Calls for Joseph	61
Pharaoh's Dreams Interpreted by Joseph	62
Pharaoh Chooses Joseph to Rule	62
The First Seven Years	62
Two Sons Born to Joseph	63
The Famine Begins	63
Joseph's Brothers Go to Egypt	63
Joseph said, "Ye Are Spies."	64
Bring Your Youngest Brother to Me	64
Brothers Depart	64
The Brothers Return to Their Father	65
Benjamin Cannot Go To Egypt	65
Out of Food, Back to Egypt	65
Judah Will Take Care of Benjamin	65
Joseph Sees Benjamin	66
Brothers to Eat Bread with Joseph	66
Joseph's Younger Brother, Benjamin	67
Joseph's Meal with His Brothers	67
The Silver Cup	67
Who Has Joseph's Cup?	68
Judah Begs To Take Benjamin's Place	68
Joseph Wept Aloud	68
Tell My Father, Jacob, to Come to Egypt	69

Pharaoh Tells Joseph to Bring His Father 69
Brothers Tell Jacob That Joseph is Alive 70
God Tells Jacob to Go See Joseph 70
Joseph Sees His Father 70
Pharaoh Meets Jacob and the Brothers 71
Jacob Blessed Pharaoh 71
Joseph's Promise to Jacob 71
Joseph Brings His Sons to Meet Jacob 71
Jacob Gives His Blessings 72
Blessing to Jacob's Sons 72
Jacob Wants to Be Buried With His People 72
Joseph Mourns His Father, Jacob 73
Let Me Go Bury My Father 73
The Brothers Carry Jacob Back to Canaan 73
Jacob is Dead and the Brothers Fear Joseph 73
Joseph said, "Fear Not." 74
Joseph's Death and Burial 74

Chapter 3 75
  Lesson 1 75
    God's Land of Promise 75
    Joseph Has Died and the Israelites Multiply 75
    The King of Egypt is Worried 75
    The Midwives Fear God 76
    The New King Wants to Get Rid of Hebrew Sons 76
    Moses Hidden 76
    Moses Put in the River 76
    Pharaoh Wants to Kill Moses 77
    God Remembers His Covenant 78
    Moses Sees the Burning Bush 78
    God Will Be With Moses 78
    Moses' Rod Turns To a Snake 79

Moses Tells God, "I Don't Speak Well." 79
God Chooses Aaron to Help Moses 79
Moses Speaks to His Father-in-law 80
Moses Speaks to Pharaoh 80
The Israelites Believe Moses 81
Moses and Aaron Visit Pharaoh 81
The Hebrew People Given More To Do 81
Pharaoh is Harsh to the People 81
The People Complain to Moses 82
Moses Prays 82
God's Renewed Covenant 82
The LORD Said to Speak to Pharaoh 83
Heads of the Fathers of the Levites 83
The Egyptians Will Know that I am the LORD 84
Aaron's Rod Swallows Their Rods 84
Pharaoh's Instructions 84
Blood, the First Plague 84
Frogs, the Second Plague 85
Pharaoh Burdened 85
Lice, the Third Plague 86
Flies, the Fourth Plague 86
Pharaoh Says Your People Can Go 86
Cattle Die, the Fifth Plague 86
Boils, the Sixth Plague 87
Warning from Moses 87
Hail, the Seventh Plague 88
Pharaoh Responds to Moses 88
Warning From Moses 88
Locust, the Eighth Plague 89
Darkness, the Ninth Plague 89
Pharaoh Warns Moses He Will Die 90

One More Plague for Egypt	90
Moses Warns of Death of the Firstborn	90
The Lamb Shall Be Without Blemish, the Passover	91
Passover to Remain a Memorial	91
Death of the Firstborn, the Tenth Plague	92
Lesson 2	**92**
God's Promised Land	92
Bones of Joseph	92
God Leads by a Pillar of Cloud and Fire	93
God Gives the Israelite People Instructions	93
The Israelites Flee , Pharaoh Pursues	93
Israelites Fear the Egyptians	93
The LORD's Salvation	94
The Red Sea Parts	94
The LORD Destroys Pharaoh's Army	95
The Women Sing With Miriam	95
The People Grumbled	95
Jethro's Wise Advice to Moses	96
Moses Called to Mount Sinai by God	96
The Ten Commandments	97
God's Instructions for a Tabernacle	98
The People Melt All Their Gold	98
Day of Atonement	99
Lesson 3	**99**
God's Promised Land	99
The LORD Commandeth to Keep Manna as a Testimony	99
God is Angry with Aaron and Miriam	100
Moses Cried for Miriam to be Healed	101
Twelve Men Chosen as Spies To Search Canaan	101
Twelve Spies Chosen	101
Spies Sent Out To Survey the Land of Canaan	101

- Search of the Land for Forty Days 102
- Israel Gets Report from the Spies 102
- Ten Spies Give a Negative Report 102
- Israelites Murmur Against Moses and Aaron 103
- Joshua and Caleb Declare that the LORD is With Them 103
- God Is Angered With Israel 103
- Israel is Punished by God 104
- Miriam's Death and Burial 104
- Moses Smote the Rock for Water 105
- Israel is Encouraged 105
- Moses Assures Joshua 106
- Moses Sees But Cannot Enter the Promised Land 106
- Moses' Death and Burial 106
- Joshua To Lead the Children of Israel 107
- Moses, the Great Prophet 107

Lesson 4 107
- The Promised Land 107
- God Speaks to Joshua 108
- Joshua Sends Men to Spy Out the Land 108
- Spies Protected by Rahab 108
- Rahab 109
- The Spies Trust Rahab 109
- Joshua Gets a Report 110
- Joshua 3 110
- The Twelve Stones Become a Memorial 111
- The Assault of Jericho and Their Fall 111
- The Spies Bring Rahab and Her Family to Safety 112
- The Destruction of Jericho 112
- Land Divided 112
- The LORD God is Levi's Inheritance 112
- Israel Hears What Joshua Has to Say 113

Do Not Turn From God 113
Joshua's Death and Burial 113
Bones of Joseph 113

Lesson 5 114
Joshua Speaks to the Children of Israel 114
An Angel Rebuked Israel 114
The People Serve the LORD 115
Joshua's Death and Burial 115
God Is Angered Toward Israel 115
God is Forgotten 116
Israel Delivered Seven Years to the Midianites 116
Gideon 117
Gideon Sees an Angel of the LORD 117
Israel is Saved by Gideon 117
Gideon Calls the Altar Jehovah-Shalom 118
The Men Want to Kill Gideon 118
God's Way of Selecting an Army 119
Gideon Gives the Men Their Weapons 119
Gideon, a Faithful Ruler 120
Gideon's Death and Burial 120
Israel Did Evil Things 120
Manoah's Request to the LORD 121
Manoah's Burnt Offering 121
Manoah and His Wife Believe They Will Die 122
Samson's Birth 122
Doings of Samson 122
Continue Reading About Samson 123
Samson Displays His Strength 123
Delilah Betrays Samson 123
Samson's Strength is Finally Revealed 124
The Philistines' Make Sport of Samson 125

Samson Talking to the Lad 125
Samson Prays to God 125
Samson's Death and Burial 126
Elkanah and His Two Wives 126
Eli Watches Hannah Pray 126
Birth of Samuel 127
Hannah Brings Samuel to Eli 127
Samuel Hears the LORD's Call 128
God Called to Samuel 128
Samuel Becomes a Prophet 129
Israel Versus the Philistines 129
Philistines Capture the Ark 129
Israel Loses the Ark in Battle 130
Eli's Death 130
Israel Rejects God 131

Chapter 4 132
  Lesson 1 132
    Saul, Son of Kish, to Become King 132
    The Meeting of Samuel and Saul 133
    Samuel Anoints Saul 133
    Saul Gets Instructions from Samuel 134
    God Gives Saul Another Heart 134
    The End for Saul's Kingdom 135
    I Samuel 14 135
    I Samuel 15 136
    Saul's Sin, God Rejects Him 136
    Jonathan, Saul's Son 136
    Saul Should Have Killed Agag 136
    Samuel Searches for a New King 137
    Samuel Chooses the Youngest Son of Jesse 137
    David Anointed 138

The LORD's Spirit Leaves Saul	138
Saul Calms When David Plays the Harp	138
The Philistines Went to Battle	139
David Takes Food to His Brothers	139
David Sees Goliath	139
David is a Brave Lad	140
David and His Sling	140
David, Son of Jesse	141
The Souls of David and Saul's Son, Jonathan	141
Saul Is Jealous and Afraid of David	142
1 Samuel 18:17-30	142
I Samuel 19	142
Michal, David's Wife, Saves Him	143
I Samuel 20:3	143
The Covenant Between Jonathan and David	144
Saul Misses David	144
Jonathan and David Depart from Each Other	144
I Samuel 24	145
Samuel's Death and Burial	145
Saul Inquires of a Woman of Spirits	145
Samuel Ascended from the Grave	146
Saul and Samuel	146
Saul's Death	147
The Philistines Disrespect Saul's Body	147
Saul's Burial	148
Lesson 2	148
A Few Highlights about King David	148
Concerning Saul's Death	148
The Young Amalekite Killed	149
David Made King of Judah	149
II Samuel 3:6-8	150

David, To Be King of Israel 150
Joab Slew Abner 151
Ishbosheth's Death 151
The Death of the Two That Killed Ishbosheth 152
David Anointed as King of Israel 152
Jerusalem Made Capital of Israel 152
A Temple for the Ark.. 153
David's Greatness and Kindness 153
David Sees Beautiful Bathsheba 154
Uriah's Death 154
A Parable from the LORD 155
David's Sin Exposed by Nathan.. 155
David Repents.. 156
David's Child Dies.. 156
David Worships the LORD After His Son Died.................................... 156
Solomon's Birth 157
II Samuel 13 157
Psalm 51 157

Lesson 3 158
David Wants a Census 158
David Repents.. 158
Don't Destroy Jerusalem 159
Araunah's Threshing Floor is Bought.. 159
Declining Health 160
Adonijah Claims Himself as King.. 160
David Assures Bathsheba 161
About Solomon.. 161
Solomon Gets Advice from David 161
David's Reign, Death, and Burial.. 162
Solomon's Wisdom.. 162
God is Pleased with Solomon's Request... 162

A Living Child and a Dead Child 163

Solomon Makes a Wise Decision 163

The Temple is Constructed 164

Solomon's Downfall 164

Solomon Builds Idols for His Wives 164

God's Anger Toward Solomon 164

Solomon's Death and Burial 165

Rehoboam 165

Rehoboam Consults with the Men 165

Abijam, Rehoboam's Son 166

Asa Loves the LORD and Follows Him 166

Nadab's Reign and Fall 166

The Temple Destroyed 167

II Chronicles 36: 21 167

Lesson 4 167

Cyrus' Proclamation 168

Coming Out of Captivity 168

Foundation Completed for the Temple 169

Jonah 1 169

Jonah 2 170

Jonah 3 170

Jonah 4 171

The Prophets 171

Isaiah 53 171

Jeremiah 172

Hosea 172

Amos 172

Amos 7: 17 172

Micah 5: 2 173

Habakkuk 2: 4 173

Zephaniah 173

Lesson 5 173
    Edom is Judged 173
    The Prophet's Warnings Ignored by Judah 174
    The People Will Serve the Babylonians Seventy Years 174
    God Will Punish the Babylonians 174
    The Action Sermons 175
    Daniel is Made Great 175
    People To Serve the Golden Image 176
    The Fiery Furnace Heated Seven Times Hotter 176
    Shadrach, Meshach, and Abednego 177
    King Darius 177
    Daniel 6: 1-3 177
    Finding Fault with Daniel 178
    The Royal Decree Signed By King Darius 178
    Daniel Prays Three Times a Day 178
    Daniel In the Lion's Den 179
    Joel, A Prophet 179
    The LORD's Givings 179
    Haggai and Zechariah 179
    Ezra and Nehemiah 180
    Malachi 180
    Four Hundred Years 180
    Esther 181
    The King Demands Queen Vashti's Presence 181
    The King Punishes His Wife 181
    Seeking A New Queen 182
    Esther Is Chosen 182
    The King Saved by Mordecai 182
    Haman Hates Mordecai 183
    Jews To Be Killed 183
    The Jews Mourn 183

- Esther and Mordecai Talk 184
- Esther's Courage 184
- Haman's Evil Plan 185
- Deeds of Mordecai Made Known 185
- Haman Tells His Wife 186
- Esther's Banquet 186
- Haman's Fate 187
- Esther Pleads for Her People 187
- Mordecai Becomes Great 187

Chapter 5 188
Lesson 1 188
- The New Testament Gospels 188
- The Bloodline of Christ 188
- Joseph 188
- Mary 189
- Jesus Was Born 189
- Micah 5:2 189
- The Wise Men Visit Jesus 190
- Journey to Egypt 190
- Joseph is Warned in a Dream 191
- Isaiah 7:14 191
- Isaiah 9:6 191
- John the Baptist 191
- The Angel Gabriel Comes to Mary 192
- Elizabeth and Mary 193
- Jesus Born in Bethlehem 193
- Hosea 11:1 194
- Luke 194
- Luke 3: 38 194
- Jesus About His Father's Business 194

Lesson 2 195

The Life of Jesus Continues	195
Jesus Baptized	196
Jesus Tempted	196
Ministry of Jesus	197
The 12 Disciples of Jesus	198
Jesus Calls the First Four Disciples	198
Just a Little Info on the First Four Disciples	198
Jesus Teaching and Healing	199
Matthew 7: 12	200
Matthew 10: 1	200
Matthew 10: 5-6	200
Jesus Talking to His Disciples	201
The Disciples Are Prepared by Jesus	201
Matthew 21: 9	202
Lesson 3	202
Garden of Gethsemane	202
The Plan to Kill Jesus	203
Alabaster Box of Ointment	203
Judas Iscariot Betrays Jesus	204
Passover Meal	204
Peter Makes a Vow to Jesus	205
Jesus Prays in Gethsemane	205
Jesus Betrayed	206
Caiaphas the High Priest	207
Peter's Denial	208
Judas Has Remorse	208
Jesus Stands Before Pilate	209
Jesus Scourged	210
Pilate Finds No Fault	210
From Pilate to Herod	211
Pilate Sees No Fault in Jesus	211

Lesson 4	212
The Crucifixion and Resurrection	212
of Our Lord Jesus Christ	212
Jesus Tortured and Mocked	213
On The Hill of Golgotha	214
Luke 23:34	214
Luke 23: 39-43	215
Jesus on the Old Rugged Cross	215
Joseph Buries Jesus in His Own Tomb	216
The Watch	216
Jesus Has Risen	217
Jesus' Appearance to Eleven Disciples	218
Doubting Thomas	218
Jesus Blessed His Disciples and Ascended into Heaven	219
Lesson 5	219
Jesus Gives Direction to His Disciples	219
Jesus Commanding the Eleven	220
Forty Days	220
Pentecost	221
Repent and Be Baptized	221
The Spirit Will Be Your Comforter	221
Leviticus 17: 11	222
Chapter 6	**223**
Lesson 1	223
Stephen	223
Stephen Accused of Blasphemy	223
Stephen Speaks to the Council	224
Stephen to Accusers	224
Stephen is Stoned	225
Revelation 2: 10	225
The Church Is Persecuted	226

Lesson 2 226

    Saul 226

    Saul is Blinded For Three Days 227

    The Lord Comes to Ananias 228

    Paul Was Also Stoned 229

    Paul's Journey to Corinth 229

    Priscilla and Aquila 230

    John's Disciples Baptized 230

    Paul's Humble Testimony 231

    Acts 22: 6-13 231

    Acts 22: 14-21 232

    Paul Heading to Rome 232

    Acts 28: 30-31 233

    Blood of Christ 233

    Newness of Life 234

    Higher Power 234

    Our Body is a Temple 234

    The Lord's Supper 235

    False Preaching 236

    Paul's Sufferings 236

    The Revelation of Jesus Christ 236

    Paul's Charge Against Peter 237

Lesson 3 238

    Barnabas 238

    Barnabas and Saul 239

    Barnabas Goes to Antioch 239

    Saul and Barnabas to Cyrus 240

    Circumcision Disputed 241

    Dispute of Paul and Barnabas 242

    Timothy 243

    Paul's Vision 243

Lydia	243
Paul and Silas	244
Prison Keepers Converted	245
Timothy	246
Paul Speaking to Timothy	246
Paul Speaking About Timothy	246
God's Mercy Toward Paul	247
Root of All Evil	247
Testimony of The Lord	248
Preach God's Word	248
Titus	249
Titus 2: 1-2	249
Qualifications for Leaders	250
Lesson 4	**251**
The Tribes Greeted	252
Trials, Temptations and Wisdom	252
James 1: 22-23	253
Don't Show Favoritism	253
Hebrews 13: 1-2	254
Faith and Works Go Together	254
Isaiah 64:6	255
Galatians 2:16	255
That Old Tongue	256
James 4: 1-12	256
Be Careful When Boasting	257
James 5:16	257
Hebrews 3:3-4	257
Hebrews 8:1	257
Hebrews 12: 28-29	258
Jude	258
Lesson 5	**259**

- 1 John 259
- 2 John 1: 1-4 260
- 2 John 1: 5-8 260
- The Doctrine of Christ 261
- 3 John 261
- John The Apostle 261
- Jesus, The Bright and Morning Star 262
- The Book of Revelation Ends 262

About the Author 264

Dedications & Acknowledgments

To my precious mother, Ruby Henderson Hand. I couldn't do this without you. She always taught her six children about the Lord. She loved Him and wanted to know her children trusted in Him, also.

To my husband, Jerry, for putting up with my many hours working on my book.

To my sweet cousin and friend, Vivian Martin, who has always been an inspiration to me and someone I have always looked up to.

To my Bible Study group. You ladies are the reason I am doing this. I love your dedication to wanting to know more about our Lord.

To my 'little sister,' Connie, for always encouraging me.

To Vicki Fletcher, for proofreading all I have written and for guiding me through my first book.

To my Lord and Savior Jesus Christ, for being with me and for opening up His word for me to understand and be able to present it in a way that anyone reading it can understand.

Thank you, and I truly love you all.

Testimonials from Group Members

Raeann Ramshaw: The Bible study has made it easier for me to learn about the Bible and I have grown in my walk with God.

Jennifer Neeley: This study gives a great overview of the Bible and makes me want to dig in more to the Word.

Vivian Martin: I participated in a group during which *A Soft Walk Through the Bible* was used as the learning guide. Being a Christian and studying the Bible has always been a way of life for me. I was truly amazed how truths were brought to my attention in this experience. It brought out truths I was never aware of while reading the Bible alone. The Holy Spirit is strongly evident in this study. I highly recommend this book for group meetings or as an individual in your quiet time with the Lord.

Mary Trenthem: I have been a student of many Bible studies in my 78 years. This one is the most memorable of all. It takes you thru the Bible from Genesis to Revelations. I enjoyed the participation of the whole group. We were learning and sharing personal stories and testimonies that related to the week's text. I highly recommend this study. Thank you, Linda, for your research and dedication while preparing this learning experience.

Teresa Milhorne: What a wonderful time of fellowship to listen, learn, and grow in our faith. All mixed with love and laughter. I like the format of this study. The highlights allow for discussion and participation from everyone.

Carolyn Henderson: Matthew 18:26 says, "For where two or three are gathered in my name, there am I." Being able to study God's Word, discuss it, and pray together as a group has been a wonderful experience. Linda's outline was presented in a way that each of us recognized new things in Scripture we had never thought of. Great Bible study and I love those ladies.

A Soft Walk Through the Bible

Chapter 1

Lessons 1 and 2
The Beginning, The Creation
Genesis 1: 1-25

John 4:24 - God is a spirit: and they that worship Him must worship Him in spirit and in truth.

In the beginning God created the heaven and the earth. The earth was without form and void; darkness was upon the face of the deep. The spirit of God moved upon the earth. God said, "Let there be light." God saw the light was good, and God divided the light from the darkness. God called the light day and the darkness He called night. The evening and the morning were the first day. God said, "Let there be a firmament in the midst of the waters and let it divide the land from the waters." God called the firmament Heaven. The evening and the morning were the second day. The dry land God called Earth; the waters he called Seas: and God saw that it was good. God said, "Let the earth bring forth grass, the herb yielding seed, and the fruit tree yielding fruit, the seed is in itself after its kind." And God saw that it was good. And the evening and the morning were the third day. God made light in the firmament of the heaven to divide the day from the night: and let them be for signs, and for seasons, and for days and years. Let them be for lights in the firmament of the heaven to give light upon the earth. God made two great lights: the greater light to rule the day and the lesser light to rule the night. He also made the stars. God set them in Heaven to give light upon the earth. And the evening and the morning were the fourth day. God said, "Let the water bring forth abundantly the moving creature and fowl that may fly above the earth in the open firmament of heaven." God created great whales, the waters brought forth abundantly, and the fowl. God blessed them and said to be fruitful and multiply in the earth. And the evening and the morning were the fifth day. God said, "Let the earth bring forth the living creature after his kind, cattle, and creeping things, and beasts of the earth after his kind." And it was so. God made the beast of the earth after his kind, and cattle after their kind, and everything that creepeth upon the earth after his kind; and God saw that it was good.

Adam
Genesis 1: 26
Genesis 2: 21-23

God breathed the breath of life into Adam—the first man to ever exist. God formed him from the dust of the earth. God made Adam in his own image. God performed the first surgery on Adam. God put Adam in a deep sleep and removed one of his ribs to create Eve, his wife. God placed Adam and Eve in His perfect world.

The Garden of Eden
Genesis 2: 16-18

Adam and Eve had all they needed. Only one restriction—they were NOT to eat of the Tree of Knowledge of Good and Evil.
God allowed Adam and Eve to make choices.

Luke 10:18

Jesus said, "I beheld Satan as lightning falls from heaven."

Satan

Satan was an angel and fell from Heaven because of pride. He desired to be God, not to be a servant of God. He was an exceedingly beautiful angel. He wanted to kick God off His throne. He wanted to take over the rule of the universe. God CAST Satan out of Heaven. Satan took on the form of a snake in the Garden of Eden.

Serpent and Eve
The Fall
Genesis 3: 1-6

The serpent said to Eve, "Hath God said, 'Ye shall not eat of every tree of the garden?'"
Eve: "We may eat of the trees of the garden. But of the tree in the midst of the garden, God said don't eat it or touch it; if you do you will die."
Serpent: "Ye shall not surely die. God knows if you eat of it, then your eyes shall be as God's, knowing good and evil."
Eve: Believing the serpent, she did eat.
It was good and pleasant to the eye. It would make one wise. Eve also gave to her husband Adam and he ate.

Lesson 3
Adam and Eve and God
Genesis 3: 7-13

Their eyes were opened. They knew they were naked. They sewed fig leaves together and made themselves aprons. They heard the voice of the LORD God walking in the garden in the cool of the day. They hid themselves amongst the trees. God called to them, "Where art thou?" Adam said, "I was afraid, because I am naked, and hid myself." God said, "Who told you, you are naked? Hast thou eaten of the tree, that I, God commanded thee not to eat or touch?" Adam: "Eve, the woman you gave me, gave it to me." God (speaking to Eve): "What is this thou hast done?" Eve: "The serpent beguiled (tricked, misled, deceived, charmed) me and I did eat."

God Speaking to the Serpent, Adam, and Eve
Genesis 3 14-20

Serpent: Because thou hast done this, thou are cursed above all cattle, and above every beast of the field. Upon thy belly shalt thou go, and the dust thou shalt eat all the days of thy life.

Eve, the Woman: God will greatly multiply thy sorrow and thy conception. In sorrow thou shall bring forth children, (birth pains), and thy desire shall be to thy husband, and he shall rule over thee.

Adam: Because you listened to your wife and ate of the tree I commanded you not to eat, the ground is cursed and in sorrow thou shalt eat of it all the days of thy life. Thorns and thistles shall it bring forth to thee. In the sweat of thy face shalt thou eat bread; till thou return unto the ground; for out of it wast thou taken, for dust thou art, and unto dust shalt thou return. Adam called his wife's name Eve because she is the mother of all living. God made Adam and Eve coats of skins and clothed them.

Adam and Eve Sent From the Garden of Eden
Genesis 3: 22-24

The LORD God said, "Man has become as one of us, to know good and evil." God sent them out of the Garden of Eden, to till the ground from where he was taken. God drove out the man. He placed Cherubims and a flaming sword which turned every way to keep the way of the tree of life at the east of the Garden of Eden.

Cherubim

Unearthly being who directly attends to God!

Flaming Sword

A flaming sword is a sword which is glowing with a flame which is produced by some supernatural power.

Children Born to Adam and Eve
Genesis 4: 1-2

After God sends Adam and Eve out of the Garden of Eden, sin continues with their children.
Adam knew Eve, his wife. They had a son, Cain.
Eve bare his brother, Abel.
Cain was a farmer or tiller of the ground.
Able was a keeper of sheep.

Cain and Able Give Offerings to God
Genesis 4: 3-7

Cain brought of the fruit of the ground an offering unto the LORD.

Verse 5: But unto Cain and his offering, God had no respect. Cain was very wroth (angry) and his countenance (appearance, his expression on his face) fell.

Abel brought of the firstlings of his flock and of the fat thereof. The LORD had respect unto Abel and his offering was accepted because it was a blood sacrifice and came from his heart.

Verse 6: God approached Cain in love and offered him a chance to correct his mistake. He warned Cain, an offering of GOOD WORKS would not be accepted. Cain was very angry and jealous of Abel.

The First Murder
Genesis 4: 8-10

When Cain and Able were in a field together, Cain talked with Abel. In a fit of anger, he killed his brother.

***Adam and Eve probably thought that the consequence of sin is death.

God and Cain

God said, "Cain, where is Abel thy brother?"

Cain replied, "I know not. Am I my brother's keeper?"
God said, "What hast thou done? The voice of thy brother's blood crieth unto me from the ground."

Cain Cursed
Genesis 4: 11-15

Cain was cursed: the earth opened her mouth to receive thy brother's blood from thy hand. Cain will be a fugitive (wander or move) and a vagabond (back and forth). Thou shalt be in the earth "Wandering Aimlessly."

God and Cain

Cain said to the LORD, "My punishment is greater than I can bear. Behold, thou hast driven me out from the face of the earth, and from Thy face shall I be hid. I shall be a fugitive and a vagabond on the earth— everyone will want to slay me!!!"

God said, "Whosoever slayeth Cain, vengeance (punish) shall be taken on him sevenfold."
The LORD set a mark upon Cain, lest any finding him should kill him.

*** Cain just killed his brother and now is blaming God for being too harsh!!!

*** This mark was another act of His grace and goodness toward Cain.

Genesis 4: 16-18

Cain went out from the presence of the LORD, and dwelt in the land of Nod, on the east of Eden.
Cain knew his wife and had a son, Enoch.
He built a city and called it Enoch after his son.
Enoch fathered Irad.
Irad fathered Methuselah.
Methuselah fathered Lamech.

Genesis 5: 28 -32

Lamech fathered Noah.
Noah fathered Shem, Ham, and Japheth.

Birth of Third Son, Seth
Genesis 4: 25-26

Adam knew his wife again and they had a third son, Seth.
Eve said, "For God hath appointed me another seed instead of Abel, whom Cain slew."

Adam's Descendants
Genesis 5

Adam— Seth. Adam lived 930 years.
Seth— Enos. Seth lived 912 years.
Enos— Cainan. Enos lived 905 years.
Cainan— Mahalalel. Cainan lived 910 years.
Mahalaleel—Jared. Mahalaleel lived 895 years.
Jared— Enoch. Jared lived 962 years.
Enoch— Methuselah. Enoch lived 365 years.

*** Enoch was the first person to walk with God.

He walked with God after he begat Methuselah.
He was raptured directly to Heaven.

Verse 24: And Enoch walked with God: and he was not, for God took him. He was the first person to be raptured directly to Heaven.

Methuselah— Lamech. Methuselah lived 969 years.
Lamech—Noah. Lamech lived 777 years.
Noah— Shem, Ham, and Japheth. Noah lived 950 years.

*** Japheth was the oldest.
Ham was the youngest.
Shem was mentioned first because it was through him that God's Messiah would come.

Genesis 9:26: And he said, "Blessed be the LORD God of Shem. And Canaan shall be his servant."

Adam and Eve's Third Son, Seth

Seth is the ancestral father of Methuselah, the longest living man and Noah, the man that built the ark and survived the great flood. Seth is the godly line of their descendants.

Genesis 6: 1-4

The global flood was ultimately caused by the ungodly line of Cain and the godly line of Seth.

The Ungodly Line of Cain and the Godly Line of Seth
Genesis 6: 1-7

They intermarried and the result brought the judgment of God upon the primeval world.

** <u>Primeval</u>: Belonging to the first or earliest age.
In the first period of life.

And God saw that the wickedness of man was great in the earth.
Man's heart was continually evil.
God's heart grieved that he had made man.
It grieved God's heart so much that he said, "I will destroy man whom I have created from the face of the earth; both man, and beast, and the creeping thing, and the fowl in the air."

Lesson Four

The Great Flood
Genesis 6: 8-13

Noah found grace in the eyes of the LORD.
Noah was a just man and perfect in his generation.
Noah walked with God.
Noah begat (fathered) three sons: Shem, Ham, and Japheth.
The earth was corrupt, filled with violence.
God looked upon the earth, it was corrupt.
God said to Noah: "The end of all flesh is come before me. The earth is filled with violence through them; and behold, I will destroy them with the earth."

Noah Builds The Ark
Genesis 6: 14-17

The ark was made of gopher wood. Its meaning is uncertain.

*** Maybe cedar or cypress.

Pitch (like tar) was used within and without.
The dimensions of the ark were more like a barge than a ship.
It was 300 cubits (about 450 feet long).
The breath of it 50 cubits (75 feet long).
The height of it 30 cubits (45 feet high).
It has about 95,700 sq. ft. on three decks.
A window was cut all the way around the ark under the roofline for light and ventilation. The door of the ark shalt thou set in the side thereof; with lower, second, and third stories shalt thou make it.
God brought a flood upon the earth to destroy all flesh.

God's Promise to Noah- The Covenant
Genesis 6: 18

God to Noah, "Thou shalt come into the ark, your sons, your wife, and your son's wives.

*** Noah- last of the pre-flood Patriarchs (the male head of a family) or (any of the very early Biblical personages regarded as the fathers of the human race).
Noah was the builder of the Ark.
Noah survived the great flood.
Noah was 600 years old when the flood began.

Noah was a righteous man, obedient, had great faith.
From Noah's three sons— Shem, Ham, and Japheth— the present world was populated.

Orders From God
Genesis 6: 19-22

God: "Bring into the ark two of every sort, to keep them alive; they shall be male and female."
And take thou unto thee of all food that is eaten."
Noah did all that God commanded him to do.

*** Web site - HolyLandSite.com
Noah's Ark Discovered Documentary
Leaving the Ark

Animals Enter the Ark
Genesis 7: 1-24

LORD to Noah, "Come thou and all thy house into the ark, thee have I seen as righteous. Of every clean beast, take to thee by sevens, the male and female. Beasts that are not clean by two, the male and female. Fowls of the air by sevens, male and female, to keep seed alive upon the face of the earth. God caused it to rain 40 days and 40 nights; every living substance that I have made will be destroyed.

*** Every time the number 40 is used in scripture, it indicates a time of testing.

Noah, his sons, his wife, and his son's wives went in.
The animals went in two and two unto Noah onto the ark, male and female as God commanded.

*** God supernaturally brought the animals to Noah.

Genesis 7:16 God shut them in.

*** God closed the door of the Ark!!!

The waters were upon the earth in 7 days.
And the waters prevailed exceedingly upon the earth; all the high hills that were under the whole heaven were covered. All the flesh died that moved upon the earth.

*** It is described as the Global Flood.

Only Noah remained alive, and they that were with him in the ark. It took the water 150 days to prevail upon the earth.

<u>Genesis 8</u>

<u>Verse 1:</u> God remembered Noah and his family. God made a wind to pass over the earth and the waters assuaged (made milder or less severe).

<u>Verse 2-3:</u> The rain stopped. The waters returned off the earth continually. And after the end of the 150 days the water abated (diminished, ended).

Noah's Ark Rests on the Mountain of Ararat
Genesis 8: 4-14

The ark rested in the seventh month of the 17th day, upon the Mountain of Ararat. The waters decrease. The 10th month on the first day, the tops of the mountains were seen. At the end of 40 days, Noah opened the window and sent forth a raven. It went to and fro until the waters were dried up. Noah sent a dove. The dove found no rest. She returned to the ark. Noah put forth his hand and pulled her into the ark. Seven days later he sends the dove out again and she comes back with an olive leaf in her mouth. Noah knew the waters were abated (diminished) from the earth. Noah sent forth the dove again in seven days and she did not return. The second month, on the 27th day, the earth dried.

God Tells Noah to Leave the Ark
Genesis 8:15-19

God spake to Noah to come out with all his family and all the living. Noah and all in the ark went forth.

Genesis 8
Verses 20-22

Noah built an altar unto the LORD. He took of every clean beast and of every clean fowl for burnt offerings. The LORD smelled a sweet savor (specific smell). The LORD said in his heart that He will never again curse the ground for man's sake, for the imagination of man's heart is evil from his youth;

neither will he smite any more of everything living, as He has done. While the earth remaineth, seed and harvest, cold and heat, summer and winter, day and night, shall not cease.

God's Blessing
Genesis 9: 1

God blessed Noah, told him and them to be fruitful and multiply and replenish the earth.

Noah and God's Covenant
Genesis 9: 8-11

God told Noah he will establish a covenant with him and his seed after him. Neither shall all flesh be cut off any more by waters of a flood and no flood will destroy the earth.

The Rainbow
Genesis 9: 12-17

God said, "I will set My bow in the cloud, and it shall be a token of a covenant between me and the earth." God said the bow shall be in the cloud and He will look upon it, and He will remember the everlasting covenant between God and every living creature of all that is upon the earth.

*** When I look at a rainbow, my thoughts are, *My LORD God is looking at the rainbow the very same time my eyes behold the rainbow.*

** *Is this not amazing?*

Lesson 5

*** Some believe the story of Job happened sometime after the flood.

Job 1: 1-3

Job lived in Uz, the exact location is uncertain, but it is usually associated with Eden. Job was perfect and upright, he feared God, and eschewed (shunned) evil. Job's life was exemplary (model person) and could not have been more. Job was a model person; he loved the LORD. Job had seven sons and three daughters. He had 7000 sheep, 3000 camels, 500 yoke of oxen, and she asses. A very great household. Job was the greatest of all men in the east.

Job 1: 4-5

His sons feasted in their house and sent for their three sisters to eat and drink with them. When the days of their feasting were gone, Job sent and sanctified (made holy) them. Job rose up early in the morning and offered burnt offerings according to the number of them all. Job said, "It may be that my sons sinned and cursed God in their hearts."

*** Job was a spiritual man and believed in only one God.

*** Sons of God means angelic beings. Satan is an angelic being. God had thrown him from heaven. He was an enemy of God. He also had access to God.

Satan Tempts Jesus
Job 1: 6-12

There was a day when the Sons of God came to present themselves before the LORD and Satan came also.
<u>LORD:</u> "Satan, whence comest thou?"
<u>Satan:</u> "From going to and fro in the earth, from walking up and down in it."
<u>LORD:</u> "Hast thou considered my servant Job? There is none like him in the earth: a perfect, upright man, he feareth God, and escheweth (shuns) evil."
<u>Satan:</u> "Doth Job fear God for nought (none or no value)? Ask God if he had put a hedge about him and his house, and all that he has. Put forth your hand now and touch all that he has."
<u>LORD to Satan:</u> "Behold, all that Job hath is in thy power; only you do not put forth thine hand on Job."
<u>Satan:</u> "Put forth your hand now and touch all that he has, and he will curse Thee to Thy face."
<u>LORD to Satan:</u> "Behold, all that Job hath is in thy power; only you do not put forth thine hand on Job."

***He cannot kill Job!!!

***Satan's power is under the control of God— always.

Afflictions of Job
Job 1: 13-19

Job's sons and daughters were eating and drinking in their eldest brother's house. The oxen were plowing, the asses feeding beside them. A messenger came and told Job, "The Sabeans fell upon them, took them away, slew the servants with the sword. I alone escaped to tell thee."

Sabeans

A nomadic Bedouin tribe known for their treachery and cruelty. They moved from place to place. They robbed other people as a means of survival.

Job 1: 16-19

While the messenger was still talking to Job, another messenger came and said, "The fire of God is fallen from Heaven, burned up the sheep, the servants, it consumed them. Only I escaped alone to tell you." While he was yet speaking, another messenger came and said, "The Chaldeans made out of three bands, fell upon the camels, carried them away, and slew the servants with the sword. Only I escaped alone to tell thee." Another messenger came and said, "Thy sons and daughters were eating and drinking wine in their eldest brother's house. A great wind from the wilderness smote the four corners of the house and fell upon them and they are all dead. I only escaped alone to tell thee."

***The Chaldeans: Also a band of nomadic marauders (someone who travels around plundering or pillaging). All of these tragic events evidently took place on the same day. Only four (4) survived to bear the bad news. Human life was lost in all four disasters.

Job Worships the LORD
Job 1: 20-22

Job arose, rent his mantle (a loose, sleeveless cloak or cape), shaved his head, fell to the ground, and worshiped. Job said,

"Naked I came from my mothers' womb, naked shall I return. The LORD gave and the LORD hath taken away; blessed be the name of the LORD." In all this, Job sinned not nor charged God foolishly.

Satan's Failure

Instead of cursing God, Job worshiped.
He lost his family and wealth.
Job remained faithful.

Job's Second Affliction by Satan
Job 2: 1-6

Again, there was a day when the Sons of God came before the LORD, and Satan came also to present himself before the LORD.
LORD: "From whence comest thou?"
Satan: "From going to and fro in the earth and from walking up and down in it."
LORD: "Hast thou considered my servant Job. There is none like him in the earth: a perfect and upright man, he feareth God, and escheweth (shuns) evil. And still he holdeth fast his integrity, although you movest Me against him, to destroy him without cause."
Satan: "Skin for skin, yea, all that a man hath will he give for life. But, put forth Thine hand now, and touch his bone and his flesh, and he will curse Thee to Thy face."
LORD: "Behold, he is in thine hand; but save his life."

Job 2: 7-8

Satan left the LORD's presence and smote Job with boils from the sole of his foot unto his crown. Job took a potsherd (a broken pottery fragment) to scrape himself and he sat down among the ashes.

Job's Wife Speaks
Job 2: 9-10

Job's wife said, "Curse God and die. Dost thou still retain thine integrity?" Job said, "Thou speakest as a foolish woman."

***Job's wife has lost a lot also. She told Job to curse God. But Job knows that good also comes from God. Sometimes God allows bad things to happen for the good to happen.

Three of Job's Friends Arrive
Job 2: 11-13

Three friends heard of all the evil that had come upon him. Their names were Eliphaz who was from Teman, Bildad the Shuhite, and Zophar the Naamathite. They had made an appointment to come and mourn and comfort Job. They saw Job from afar off and knew him not. They lifted up their voices and wept. And they rent everyone his mantle and sprinkled dust upon their heads toward heaven. They sat with him upon the ground seven days and seven nights. None spoke a word to him for they saw that his grief was very great.

Job Cursed His Birth
Job 3: 1-3

After the seven (7) days, Job opened his mouth and cursed the day he was born. Job said, "Let the day perish wherein I was born, and the night in which it was said, 'There is a man child conceived.'"

Job Longs for Death
Job 3: 20-24

Wherefore is light given to him that is in misery, and life unto the bitter soul, which longs for death, but it cometh not.

***Job never cursed God.

***The LORD not only restored Job's fortunes, but God also restored them in abundance.

Tower of Babel
Genesis 11: 1-9

A united human race in the generations following the Great Flood, all were speaking a single language. They agreed to build a city and tower tall enough to reach heaven. God, observing their city and tower, confused their speech so that they no longer understand each other, and scattered them around the world.

***There is no mention in Genesis of any destruction of the tower. The people simply scattered all over the face of the earth.

Chapter 2

Lesson 1

After the Tower of Babel, God scattered the nations so people are everywhere. A man named Terah lives in a town called Ur.

Shem – Noah's son is a descendant to Terah and Abram.
Terah is the father of Abram (Abraham), Haran, and Nahor II. One of his grandchildren was Lot, whose father Haran, died in Ur.

Genesis 9: 20-24

Noah planted a vineyard. He drank wine and was drunk and uncovered in his tent. Ham saw his father's nakedness and told his two brothers.
Shem and Japheth took a garment, went in backward, and covered their father, Noah. When Noah awoke, he knew what his younger son had done.
Noah said, "Cursed be Canaan. Canaan was Ham's son." Noah blessed Shem and Japheth for covering his nakedness. Several generations later, Terah was born in Shem's family line.

Genesis 11:31-32

Terah took Abram, his son, and Lot, the son of Haran, his brother's son, and Sarai, his daughter-in-law, his son Abram's wife. They went from Ur to go into the land of Canaan, they came unto Haran and dwelt there.

Sarai

<u>Sarai</u> came from Ur with Abram. Sarai was Abram's wife and also his half-sister. She was barren (unable to have children). Sarai is the daughter of Abram's father, but not his mother. God promised Abram many children, Sarai didn't believe she would ever have children.

Genesis 12: 1-4

The LORD told Abram to get out of thy country, from thy kindred, thy father's house, unto a land I will show thee. I will bless them that bless thee and curse him that curseth thee. Abram departed with Lot, his brother's son, and they went forth unto the LORD of Canaan.

Abram Deceives the Egyptians
Genesis 12: 10-16

There was a famine and Abram went down into Egypt to stay for a time; for the famine was severe in the land. When they came near to Egypt, he told Sarai, "Tell the Egyptians that you are my sister, that it may be well with me for thy sake, and my soul shall live because of thee. And when they came into Egypt, the Egyptians saw that Sarai was very fair to look upon. The princes of Pharaoh saw her and took her to Pharaoh's house. And he treated Abram well for her sake.

Genesis 12: 17-20

The LORD sent plagues upon Pharaoh because of Sarai. Pharaoh called Abram and said, "What have you done? Why did you not tell me she is your wife? Take your wife and go thy way." They sent Abram, his wife, and all they had away.

Genesis 13: 1-4

Abram, his wife Sarai, Lot, and all they had left Egypt. Abram was very rich. He went on his journey from the South even to Bethel unto the place where his tent had been at the beginning and Hai; unto the place of the altar, which he had made there at the first. There Abram called on the name of the LORD.

Abram and Lot Part Ways
Genesis 13: 5-13

Lot also had plenty. The land was not able to bear them both. There was strife between the herdsmen of Abram and Lot.
<u>Abram to Lot</u>: "Let there be not strife between us. The whole land is before thee. If thou will take the left, then I will go to the right, or if you go to the right, I will go to the left."
Lot saw the plain of Jordan was well watered everywhere before the LORD destroyed Sodom and Gomorrah. Lot chose all the plain of Jordan. They separated from each other. Abram dwelled in the land of Canaan. Lot pitched his tent toward Sodom. But the men of Sodom were wicked and sinners before the LORD.

The Covenant Renewed by God
Genesis 13: 14-18

The LORD said to Abram after he separated from Lot, "Lift up thine eyes, and look from the place where thou art: north, south, east, and westward. For all the land thou see, to thee will I give to you and thy seed forever. Abram built an altar unto the LORD.

Lot, Abram's Nephew

Abram's nephew came with him to Canaan. They separated their belongings and went their separate ways. Lot's selfish choice of the Jordan Valley and his weakness in pitching his tent toward Sodom led to tragic consequences. He soon moved to Sodom.

Downfall of Sodom and Gomorrah
Genesis 18: 19

The LORD informed Abraham that the sin of Sodom and Gomorrah is so grievous (the men were homosexuals) that He is going to destroy them.
Abraham pleads with God to have mercy on them because of his nephew, Lot, and his family.

Abraham Asks God to Spare Sodom
Genesis 18: 23-33

Abraham said to the LORD, "Wilt thou also destroy the righteous with the wicked? Will you spare the place if I can find 50 righteous?

The LORD said, "If you find 50 righteous then I will spare it." Then Abraham asked if 45, then 40, then 30, then 20, then 10 would save them.
Then God said, "I will not destroy it for ten's sake." The LORD could not find 10 righteous.

Lot Sees Two Angels
Genesis 19: 1-3

Two angels visit Sodom. Lot saw them; he rose up to meet them and bowed himself with his face toward the ground. He asked them to stay all night, wash their feet, rise up early, and go on their way.
They said, "Nay; we will abide in the street all night."
Lot pressed upon them greatly, then they turned to him and entered into the house. Lot made them a feast, baked unleavened bread, and they did eat.

Evil Men Call Out to Lot
Genesis 19: 4-11

Before the angels laid down, the evil men came around the house, young and old. They called to Lot, "where are the men which came unto you tonight? Bring them to us that we may know them."
Lot went out and shut the door after him and said, "Do not be so wicked. I have two daughters that are virgins. Let me bring them to you. Do unto them as is good in your eyes. Only unto these men, do nothing."

They didn't want the daughters, they wanted the men, and they came near to break down the door. But the men (angels) pulled Lot into the house and shut the door. They smote the men at the door with blindness.

*** I question in my mind, *How can a father offer his daughters to these evil men?* I have to ask myself, "What was he thinking?"

Lot's Family Flees Sodom
Genesis 19: 12-26

The Angels said to Lot, "Bring your family out of this place, for we will destroy it. The LORD has sent us to destroy it. When the morning arose, the angels told Lot to take his wife and two daughters, lest they be consumed in the iniquity of the city. When Lot lingered, the men laid hold upon his hand, his wife, and two daughters. The LORD was merciful to them. They were told, "Escape for thy life; do not look back, escape to the mountain lest thou be consumed." They were instructed to flee to the Small City of Zoar, without looking back. Lot's wife disobeyed. She looked back and she turned into a pillar of salt.

Destruction of Sodom and Gomorrah
Genesis 19: 24-29

The LORD rained brimstone and fire from out of heaven. He overthrew them all. The next morning Lot looked toward Sodom and Gomorrah and saw the smoke of the country as the smoke of a furnace. And it came to pass, when God destroyed the cities, God remembered Abraham, and sent Lot out of the mist of the overthrown, when he overthrew the cities in which Lot dwelt

Lot's Daughters Have Sons
Genesis 19: 30-38

Lot was afraid to stay in Zoar. He dwelt in the mountain in a cave with his two daughters. The oldest daughter said to the younger, "Our father is old and there is not a man in the earth to come unto us."
So, they gave their father wine and they both went in and laid with him to preserve the seed of their father. The oldest went in the first night and the youngest went the next night. They both conceived. And Lot perceived (knew not) when they laid down nor when they arose. The first born had a son named Moab and he is the father of Moabites. The younger had a son named Benammi, the same is the father of the children of Ammon unto this day.

***Again, I can't grasp even the thought of lying with my father!!!

Lesson 2
Abram and Sarai

Abram tells Sarai, "God has told me He is going to open your barren womb." Several years pass and Sarai doesn't get pregnant.

***They didn't wait upon the LORD; they took matters into their own hands.

Sarai told him to go into her maidservant, Hagar. Because she worked for Sarai, the child would be hers (Sarai). Sarai thought, *Since I can't have children, this is the only way to have a child.*

Genesis 16

Sarai had a handmaid, an Egyptian, named Hagar. Sarai said unto Abram, "I can't have children, so go into Hagar, that I may obtain children by her."
Abram hearkened to the voice of Sarai. They had lived in the land of Canaan 10 years. Hagar conceived and she mocked Sarai. Sarai despised Hagar and she said unto Abram, "My wrong be upon thee when she conceived. I was despised in her eyes. The LORD judge between me and thee." Abram told Sarai to do with her as she pleases. Sarai dealt hardly (harshly) with her. Hagar fled from her face.

Hagar

The angel of the LORD found Hagar by a fountain of water in the wilderness in the way to Shur (probably of the Arabian desert, on the north-eastern border of Egypt).
The angel asked Hagar, "Where did you come from and where are you going?"
Hagar said, "I flee from Sarai, my mistress."
The angel instructed, "Return to her, submit thyself under her hands. I will multiply thy seed exceedingly that it shall not be numbered for multitude. Behold, you are with child, a son, and you shall call his name Ishmael because the LORD has heard your affliction (pain, grief, misery). He will be a wild man; his hand will be against every man, and every man's hand against him.

Birth of Ishmael

Hagar bare Abram a son and called his name, Ishmael.
Abram was fourscore and six years old (86).

Genesis 17: 18-22

Abram said unto God, "O that Ishmael might live before thee." God said, "I have heard thee: behold, I have blessed him. He will be fruitful and will multiply; 12 princes shall he begat (father) and I will make him a great nation. But my covenant will I establish with Isaac, which Sarai shall bear unto thee at this set time in the next year. God left and went up from Abraham.

Covenant Between God and Abram
Genesis 17

God appeared to Abram when he was 99 years old and said, "I am the Almighty God; walk before me and be thou perfect. And I will make my covenant between Me and thee and will multiply thee exceedingly." Abram fell on his face and God talked with him saying, "As for Me, behold, My covenant is with thee, and thou shalt be a father of many nations."

From Abram to Abraham
Genesis 17:5-15

God changed <u>Abram's</u> name to <u>Abraham</u>, for a father of many nations have I made thee. God said, "I will give thee and thy seed after thee the land of Canaan for an everlasting possession and I will be their God. This is My covenant, which ye shalt keep and your seed after thee: every man child among you shall be circumcised and ye shall circumcise the flesh of your foreskin and it shall be a token of the covenant between Me and you and he that is eight days old shall be circumcised. All in your generations, born in the house, bought with money of any stranger, which is not thy seed. The uncircumcised man child whose flesh of his foreskin is not circumcised, that soul shall be cut off from his people; he hath broken my covenant. As for <u>Sarai</u> thy wife, her name shall be <u>Sarah</u>."

God's Promise of a Son
Genesis 17: 16-19

God said, "I will bless Sarah and give her a son, and she shall be a mother of all nations; kings of people shall be of her." Abraham fell upon his face and laughed. "I am a 100 years old and Sarah is 90 years old."
God said, "Sarah thy wife shall bear a son and call his name Isaac, and I will establish My covenant with him for an everlasting covenant, and his seed."

Circumcision of Abraham's House

Abraham was 99, Ishmael was 13, they were circumcised the same day. And all the men were circumcised.

Three Visitors From Heaven
Genesis18: 1-8

He sat in the tent door in the heat of the day. He saw three men standing by him. He ran to meet them and bowed himself toward the ground. He said, "My Lord, if I have found favor in they sight, pass not away, I pray thee, from they servant. Let me wash your feet and you can rest under the tree. Abraham prepared a meal for them. God was one of the guest of Abraham. Hebrews 13:1-2 says Let Brotherly love continue. Be not forgetful to entertain strangers: for thereby some have entertained angels.

The Promise that Made Sarah Laugh to Herself
Genesis 18: 9-15

<u>Angelic Visitors ask Abraham:</u> "Where is Sarah thy wife?"
<u>Abraham:</u> "Behold, in the tent."
<u>Angelic Visitor:</u> "Thy wife Sarah shall have a son."
Sarah heard it from the tent door. Sarah and Abraham were old. Sarah laughed within herself. The LORD said, "Is anything too hard for the LORD? At the time appointed, I will return unto thee, according to the time of life, and Sarah shall have a son."
Sarah denied laughing, for she was afraid.
And he said, "Nay; but thou didst laugh."

*** The name Isaac means laugh/will laugh.

Isaac Born to Abraham and Sarah
Genesis 21

Abraham gave the name Isaac to the son Sarah bore him. When his son Isaac was eight days old, Abraham circumcised him as God commanded him. Abraham was a hundred years old when his son was born to him.

Abraham's Son to Be a Sacrifice
Genesis 22: 1-8

God did tempt (test or provoke) Abraham. God said, "Abraham!!" And Abraham said, "Behold, here I am."
God said, "Take your only son whom thou lovest, to Moriah (in the general area that included the hills on which Solomon later built his temple in Jerusalem) and offer him there for a burnt offering upon one of the mountains which I tell thee of."

James 1:13 Let no man say when he is tempted, I am tempted of God: for God cannot be tempted with evil, neither tempteth he any man.

God knew that Abraham trusted and did fear Him. God knew what Abraham would do in the end! Abraham rose up early in the morning, saddled his ass (donkey), took two young men, his son Isaac, and wood for a burnt offering. He went to the place God told him. The third day, Abraham saw the place a far off. He told the young men to stay with the ass. He and Isaac will go to worship and come again to them. Abraham laid the wood upon his son, took the fire in his hand, and a knife, and they went together.
Isaac said, "Behold the fire and wood, but where is the lamb for the burnt offering?"
Abraham said, "My son, God will provide himself a lamb for the burnt offering."

God Provides a Sacrifice for Abraham
Genesis 22: 9-19

They came to the place. Abraham built an altar, laid the wood, and he bound Isaac, and laid him upon the altar. Abraham stretched forth his hand to slay Isaac. An angel of the LORD called unto him out of Heaven and said, "Abraham, Abraham." And he said, "Here am I." "Lay not thine hand upon the lad, do nothing to him. I know thou fearest God. Seeing thou has not withheld thy son." Abraham looked and in the thicket a ram was caught by his horns. He took the ram and offered it instead of Isaac. And Abraham called the name of that place Jehovah-Jireh (God will provide).
As it is said today, "In the mount of the LORD it shall be seen."

God Blesses Abraham
Genesis 22:15-19

The LORD called unto Abraham out of heaven a second time. "By myself have I sworn, because you have done this thing, and not withheld thy son, I will bless thee, and in multiplying I will multiply thy seed as the stars in heaven and the sand upon the seashore and thy seed shall possess the gate of his enemies. In thy seed shall all nations of the earth be blessed." So, Abraham returned unto his young men. They rose up together and went to Beersheba and Abraham dwelt there.

Lesson 3

Rebekah, Esau, and Jacob

***It is heavy on my heart today that I share this: God's spirit is all around us! Are we sure God is satisfied with our behavior?

Sarah Dies and is Buried
Genesis 23:1-2

Sarah was 127 years old when she died. Abraham came to mourn, and he did weep for her. Abraham buried Sarah, his wife, in the cave of the field of Machpelah, the same is Hebron in the land of Canaan.

Abraham Sends His Servant to Find a Wife for Isaac
Genesis 24: 1-9

The LORD blessed Abraham in all things. He was old and well stricken in age. Abraham said to his eldest servant of his house that ruled over all that he had, "Put thy hand under my thigh, swear by the LORD, the God of Heaven, and the God of earth, that you will not take a wife from the Canaanites for my son Isaac. But go to my country, to my kindred, and take a wife for him."

The servant asked, "What if the woman is not willing to come to Canaan? Do I need to take your son there to the land you come from (Ur of the Chaldees)?"

Abraham said, "Bring not my son thither again. God promised he would give me seed of my land; he shall send his angel before thee, and thou shall take a wife unto my son from thence. If the woman is not willing to come, then thou shalt be clear from this oath." Then the servant put his hand under Abraham's thigh and swore to him about this matter.

The Servant Prays for Isaac's Wife
Genesis 24: 10-14

The servant took ten camels and departed to the city of Nahor. He made his camels kneel down by a well of water in the evening, the time the women go out to draw water. The servant prayed, "O LORD God, master of Abraham, I pray, send me good speed today and show kindness unto my master Abraham." As he stood there, the daughters of the men of the city came out to draw water. He said to the LORD, "Let it come to pass, the damsel to whom I shall say, 'Let down thy pitcher that I may drink' and she will say, 'Drink, and I will give thy camels drink also,' then I will know Thou has appointed her for Thy servant Isaac, and I will know Thou has shown kindness to my master Abraham."

Rebekah
Genesis 24: 15-28

Before the servant had finished speaking, Rebekah came out with her pitcher upon her shoulder. (She is the daughter of Abraham's brother, Bethuel). Rebekah was very fair to look upon, a virgin. She went down to the well, filled her pitcher, and came up. The servant ran to meet her, "Let me drink a little of your water." Rebekah said, "Drink my lord." She gave him drink. Then after she had done giving him drink, she said, "I will draw water for thy camels also." She emptied her pitcher into the trough for the camels. He wondered if the LORD had made his journey prosperous or not. After the camels finished drinking, the man took a golden earring and two bracelets for her hands. And asked, "Whose daughter art thou? Is there room in your father's house for us to lodge in?" She said, "I am the daughter of Bethuel. We have both straw and provender (dry food, such as hay), and enough room to lodge in." The servant bowed down his head and worshiped the LORD. He said, "Blessed be the LORD God of my master Abraham, who hath not left destitute my master of his mercy and truth. I, being in the way, the LORD led me to the house of my master's brethren." And the damsel ran and told them of her mother's house these things. Rebekah's brother Laban prepared the house and room for the camels.

The Servant Tells Why He Came
Genesis 24: 32-49

The servant said, "I will not eat until I have told you why I have come. I am Abraham's servant. The LORD has blessed him greatly, he has become great. He has flocks, herds, silver, gold, men servants, maid servants, camels, and asses. His wife Sarah bore a son to him when she was old. Unto him hath he given all that he hath. He made me swear that Isaac would not take a wife from the Canaanites in the land where I dwell. But that I would go unto his father's house, his kindred, and take a wife for his son. I asked my master, "What if the woman will not follow me? I prayed for the LORD to show me, that when the virgin comes to draw water, and I say to her to give me drink, and she says she will give me drink and water my camels also. And behold, before I had done speaking, Rebekah came forth from the well and drew water for my camels also. She told me who her father is. I put the earring upon her face and bracelets on her hands. Then I bowed my head and worshiped the LORD God of my master Abraham, which led me to my master's brother. Now tell me, if ye will deal kindly and truly with my master. And if not, tell me that I may turn to the right hand or to the left."

Bethuel, Rebekah's Father, Says She Can Go
Genesis 24: 50-57

Laban, her brother, and Bethuel, her father, said, "This is from the LORD. We can't speak to you bad or good. Let Rebekah go and be the wife of your master's son, Isaac." When he heard these words, he bowed himself to the earth and worshiped the LORD. He brought jewels of silver and gold and raiment to Rebekah. He also gave to her brother (Laban) and her mother precious things.

The Servant Said, "Let Us Go to My Master."
Genesis 24:54-57

They ate and drank, they tarried all night, they rose up early and said, "Send me away unto my master." Her brother and mother said, "Let Rebekah abide with us at least 10 days, then she shall go." He said, "hinder me not that I may go to my master." They said, "We will call the damsel and ask her."

Rebekah Leaves
Genesis 24: 58-61

They call Rebekah and she said, "I will go." They sent Rebekah away with her nurse, the servant, and his men. They blessed Rebekah. She rode upon the camels, and they took her away.

Rebekah Becomes Isaac's Wife
Genesis 24: 62-67

Isaac went out to the field to meditate. He lifted up his eyes and saw the camels coming. Rebekah lifted her eyes and when she saw Isaac, she got off the camel. She asked the servant, "What man is this that walketh in the field to meet us?" He said, "It is my master." Then she took her veil and covered herself. The servant told Isaac all the things he had done. And Isaac brought Rebekah unto Sarah's tent and he took Rebekah, she became his wife, he loved her. Isaac was comforted after his mother's death.

Abraham's Gifts to His Descendants
Genesis 25: 1-6

Abraham again took a wife, Keturah. They had sons and grandsons. Abraham gave all that he had to Isaac. He gave unto the sons of his concubines gifts and sent them away from his son Isaac.

Abraham's Death and Burial
Genesis 25: 7-11

Abraham was 175 years old. He gave up the ghost and died at a good old age, an old man. His sons, Isaac and Ishmael, buried him in the cave of Machpelah in the field of Ephron. Abraham and Sarah were buried together. After the death of Abraham, God blessed Isaac; and Isaac dwelt by the well Lahai Roi.

Rebekah Has Twins
Genesis 25: 24-28

When Rebekah delivered, behold, there were twins. The first came out red all over like a hairy garment; and they called him Esau. After that, his brother came out, and his hand took hold of Esau's heel, and his name is Jacob. Isaac was 60 years old. The boys grew. Esau was a cunning hunter, a man of the fields. Jacob was a plain man, dwelling in tents. Isaac loved Esau because he ate his venison. But Rebekah loved Jacob. (Jacob means, heel grabber, also deceiver)

Esau Bargains With Jacob
Genesis 25: 29-36

Esau came from the field, and he was faint. Jacob had made pottage.
Esau said, "Feed me, I pray thee."
Jacob said, "Sell me this day thy birthright."
Esau said, "Behold, I am at the point to die. What profit shall this birthright do to me?"
Jacob said, "Swear to me this day."
Esau did swear and sold his birthright to Jacob. Jacob gave Esau bread and pottage. Esau ate and drank, rose up, and went his way. Esau despised his birthright.

*** He considered the responsibilities and honors unimportant.

Isaac Wants to Bless Esau
Genesis 27: 1-5

Isaac was old, his eyes dim, so that he could not see. He called Esau, his eldest son and said, "My son." And Esau said, "Behold, here am I." Isaac said, "I am old. I know not the day of my death. Go out with thy weapons and thy bow. Go to the field and take me some venison. Make me a savory meat that I love, bring it to me, that I may eat; that my soul may bless thee before I die."
Rebekah heard Isaac talking to Esau.

The Plot Against Esau
Genesis 27: 6-17

Rebekah told Jacob what she heard. "Now listen and obey my voice. Go now to the flock, fetch two good kids of the goats. I will make them savory meat for thy father that he loves. And you, Jacob, will take it to thy father that he may bless you before his death. Jacob said, "But Esau is a hairy man, and I am a smooth man. My father will feel me, and he will see me as a deceiver and bring a curse upon me, not a blessing." His mother said, "Upon me be thy curse. Obey my voice, go fetch them to me." Jacob brought them back and his mother made a savory meat. She took Esau's goodly raiments and put them on Jacob. She put skins of the kid goats upon his hands and the smooth of his neck. She gave the meat and bread she prepared unto the hand of Jacob.

Jacob Lies to His Father
Genesis 27: 18-22

Jacob came unto his father and said, "I am Esau. Arise and eat of my venison that thy soul may bless me." Isaac said, "How did you find it so quickly?" Jacob said, "Because the LORD thy God brought it to me." Isaac said, "Come near, that I may feel thee, whether thou be my son Esau or not." Jacob went near him. He felt him and said, "The voice is Jacob's voice, but the hands are of Esau."

Isaac Believes Jacob is Esau
Genesis 27: 23-29

Isaac blessed Jacob because his hands were hairy as his brother Esau's. He said, "Art thou Esau?" Jacob said, "I am." Isaac ate his son's venison and blessed him. His father said, "Come near now and kiss me, my son." He smelled him and it was the smell of Esau. Isaac said, "God give thee of the dew of heaven, fatness of the earth, plenty of corn and wine. Let the people serve thee; and bow down to thee. Be lord over thy brethren and let thy mother's sons bow down to thee. Cursed be everyone that curseth thee and blessed be he that blesseth thee."

Jacob Received the Blessing
Genesis 27: 30-33

Jacob had just received the blessing and left. His brother Esau came in with his savory meat to give his father. Esau told his father to get up and eat that he might bless him. Isaac trembled and said, "Who is this? I have already blessed him that brought me venison before you came. Yea and he shall be blessed."

Esau Weeps
Genesis 27: 34-40

When Esau heard his father's words, he cried with a great and bitter cry. He said, "Bless me, even me, also, O my father." Isaac said, "Your brother came and hath taken away thy blessing." Esau said, "He has taken away my birthright and now he has taken my blessing. Hast thou not reserved a blessing for me?" Isaac said, "Esau, I have made him thy lord. I have given him all." Esau said, "Hast thou but one blessing, my father? Bless me, my father." And Esau lifted up his voice and wept.

Revenge Planned by Esau
Genesis 27: 41-46

The days of mourning for my father are at hand. Esau said in his heart that he hated Jacob. He said he will slay his brother. These words were told to Rebekah, and she told Jacob that Esau is planning to kill you. "Obey my voice, arise, and flee to Laban my brother in Haran. Stay with him a few days until Esau's fury turns away, until his anger turns away from thee. I will send and fetch thee." Rebekah said to Isaac her husband, "I am weary. If Jacob takes a wife from the daughters of Heth, the Hittite women, my life will not be worth living." She used that as an excuse for Isaac to send Jacob away so Esau wouldn't slay Jacob.

No Wife from Canaan for Jacob
Genesis 28: 1-9

Isaac called to Jacob, blessed him, and said, "Thou shall not take a wife of the daughters of Canaan. Go to Padanaram, house of Bethuel thy mother's father. Take thee a wife from thence of the daughters of Laban, thy mother's brother." Isaac sent him away. Esau saw that Isaac blessed Jacob and sent him away to take a wife from Padanaram, and that Jacob obeyed his father and mother. Esau saw that the daughters of Canaan didn't please his father. Esau went unto Ishmael and took a wife which he had: Mahalath, daughter of Ishmael, Abraham's son, the sister of Nebajoth to be his wife.

Ladder to Heaven
Genesis 28: 10-19

Jacob went from Beersheba toward Haran. He came upon a place and stayed all night. He took stones and made a pillow and laid down to sleep. He dreamed about a ladder that reached from earth into heaven and the angels of God ascending and descending on it. Behold, the LORD stood about it, and said, "I am the LORD God of Abraham thy father, and the God of Isaac, the land where on you lay, I will give it to you and your seed. And thy seed shall be as the dust of the earth. Thou shall spread about to the west, east, north, and south. In thy seed shall all the families of the earth be blessed. I am with thee, will keep thee in all places, will bring you again into this land. I will not leave thee until I have done that which I have spoken." Jacob woke up and said, "Surely the LORD is in this place; and I know not." He was afraid and said, "How dreadful is the place! This is none other but the house of God, and this is the gate to heaven." Jacob rose up early and poured oil on the rocks he had made for a pillow. He called the name of that place Bethel.

Jacob's Pledge to God
Genesis 28: 20-22

Jacob vowed, "If God be with me and give me bread and raiment, then so that I come again to my father's house in peace, then shall the LORD be my God. And this stone, which I have set for a pillar, shall be God's house. And of all that thou shalt give me, I will surely give the tenth unto thee.

***Bethel means House of God. It was the name Jacob gave it, <u>the place where he met God.</u> It was called Luz before.

Jacob and Rachel
Genesis 29: 1-13

Jacob journeyed and came unto the land of the east. A well was in the field and a stone They watered the flocks and they put the stone back on the well's mouth. Jacob spoke to them and asked where they were from. They said, "Haran." He asked if they knew Laban and they said they did know him, and he is well. Behold Rachel his daughter comes with sheep. When Jacob saw Rachel, he went near, rolled the stone from the well's mouth and watered the flock. Jacob kissed Rachel and lifted up his voice and wept. Jacob told Rachel who he was, and she ran and told her father. Laban ran to meet Jacob, embraced him, kissed him, and brought him to his house.

Jacob Works for Laban
Genesis 29:14-31

Jacob stayed a month, and he told Laban, "I will work for you." Laban had two daughters: Leah was the oldest and Rachel was the youngest. Leah was tender eyed (gentle or weak eyed). Rachel was beautiful. Jacob loved Rachel and said, "I will serve thee seven years for Rachel." Laban agreed. Jacob did serve seven years and he said to Laban, "Give me my wife, for the days are fulfilled that I may go in unto her." Laban made a feast and brought Leah, his oldest daughter, unto Jacob. In the morning Jacob said, "What is this you have done to me? I served seven years for Rachel, and you deceived me." Laban said, "I cannot give you the younger one first. Serve with me another seven years and you can have Rachel." He gave him Rachel after he completed the wedding week with Leah. Then he went into Rachel. He loved her more than Leah.

When God saw Leah was hated, he opened her womb. Rachel was barren.

***I had always thought Jacob had to work another seven years before he could have Rachel as his wife. But the above writing reads, "he gave him Rachel after he completed the wedding week with Leah." So this could be a good discussion for a study group.

Leah Has Children and Their Maidservants

Leah bore him four sons and Rachel was envious. She said unto Jacob, "Give me children or else I die." Jacob was angered against Rachel and said, "Am I in God's stead who hath withheld from thee the fruit of the womb?" Rachel said, "Go in unto my maid, Bilhah, that she may bear, that I will have children by her." So, Jacob went in unto Bilhah. She had a son called Dan. Then she had another son called Naphtali. When Leah saw all this, she took her maid, Zilpah, and also gave her to Jacob. She bore a son called Gad. Then she had a second son called Asher. Leah conceives again and ends up having a total of six sons, then she had a daughter Dinah.

Leah's First Four Sons
Genesis 29: 32-35

<u>Reuben:</u> Hoping Jacob would love her.
<u>Simeon:</u> Because the LORD knew she was hated.
<u>Levi:</u> Felt her husband would be joined unto her.
<u>Judah:</u> She praised the LORD.

Judah

Judah was the fourth son of Jacob and Leah. He was the ancestral forerunner to Christ Himself. He was the founder of the Tribe of Judah of the Israelites. The Jews are named and mostly descendants from the Tribe of Judah. King David belonged to this tribe.

*** We will study about David in Chapter 4.

*** Some other prophets that belonged to the Tribe of Judah: Isaiah, Amos, Habakkuk, Joel, Micah, and Obadiah.

Revelations 5:5 Jesus is called the Lion of the Tribe of Judah.

God Remembered Rachel and She Conceived
Genesis 30: 22-24

God remembered Rachel and opened her womb. She conceived, had a son, and called him, Joseph.
Jacob loved Joseph more than any of his children.

Jacob Wants to Leave
Genesis 30: 28-43

After Joseph was born, Jacob wanted to leave and go back to his country. He told Laban to give him his wives and children. "For you know my service which I have done for thee." Laban said, "I have found favor in your eyes. The LORD has blessed me for thy sake. Tell me your wages?" Jacob said, "You know all I have done, all you have has increased, and the LORD has blessed you since my coming. I will pass through the flock. I will pick the spotted cattle, goats, and sheep, and such shall be my hire." Laban said, "Behold, I would it might be according to thy word." Jacob took the stronger cattle and left Laban the feeble cattle. Jacob increased exceedingly. He had much cattle, maidservants, and menservants. He had very much.

Jacob Listens to God
Genesis 31

Laban's sons told him that Jacob hath taken away all that was our father's and then Laban did not feel the same toward Jacob. And the LORD said to Jacob, "Return unto the land of thy fathers and your kindred; and I will be with you." Laban did pursue Jacob, but God told Laban in a dream, "Speak not to Jacob either good or bad." Laban did overtake Jacob and said, "What have you done, stolen from me, taken away my daughters?" Jacob reminded Laban about all the years he worked for him: 14 for Leah and Rachel and six for the cattle. Jacob and Laban did come to an understanding. They built a pillar out of stones. Laban said to Jacob, "Behold, this heap and this pillar (heap of witness). It be a witness: I will not pass over this heap unto thee and thou shalt not pass over the heap unto me for harm.

*** There is no more mention of Laban in Genesis.

Jacob Goes on His Way
Genesis 32: 1-11

Jacob went on his way; the angels of God met him. When Jacob saw them, he said, "This is God's host." And he named that place Mahanaim.

*** Mahanaim is believed to be about 10 miles east of the Jordan River.

Jacob sent word to his brother, Esau, that he wants to come back home, he has plenty, and hopes he may find grace in his sight. The messengers returned and said, "Your brother comes to meet you and 400 men with him."
Jacob was afraid. He divided the people, flocks, herds, and camels into two bands. If Esau comes and smites one, then the other shall escape.

***Bands: A company of persons or animals joined together.

Jacob Asks God for Deliverance
Genesis 32: 9-18

Jacob prayed to God, who said to him, "Return to thy country and thy kindred and I will deal well with you." Jacob said, "I am not worthy of your mercies. I pass over this Jordan and now I have become two bands. Deliver me, I pray thee, from my brother Esau. I fear him, that he might smite me and the mother of my children. You said you will do good to me and make my seed as the sand of the sea."

Jacob Sends Gifts to Esau

Jacob had delivered to Esau goats, ewes, rams, camels with their colts, bulls, and she asses with their foals. He said, "Tell them his servant Jacob is behind them."

Jacob and an Angel
Genesis 32: 24-27

Jacob was left alone. And there was a man that wrestled with him until the breaking of the day. And when he saw that he prevailed not against him, he touched the hollow of his thigh and the hollow of Jacob's thigh. Jacob's thigh was out of joint as he wrestled with him. He said, "I will not let you go except you bless me." The angel asked, "What is your name?"
And he said, "Jacob."

Lesson 4

Jacob's Name is Changed
Genesis 32: 28-32

God changed Jacob's name to Israel. God blessed Jacob that day. And Jacob called the name of the place Peniel, for I have seen God face to face and my life is preserved. He touched the hollow of Jacob's thigh. Jacob was left with a permanent limp.

The Twins Meet Again
Genesis 33: 1-16

Jacob looked and saw his brother Esau coming with 400 men. Jacob divided the children of Leah and Rachel and the handmaids. Jacob bowed himself to the ground seven times until he came to Esau. And Esau ran to Jacob, embraced, and kissed him and they wept. Esau asked, "Who is with you?" Jacob showed him all his children by the handmaidens, then Leah and Rachel last. They each bowed to Esau. Jacob said, "The children which God has so graciously given to me." Esau said, "All this you have brought me, you keep my brother. I have enough." Jacob said, "Nay, if I have found grace in your sight, then receive my present." Esau said, "God hath dealt graciously with me and I have enough." And Jacob urged him, and he took it. Esau said, "Let us take our journey, and I will go before thee." Jacob said, "You go ahead. I have small children that are tender, flocks and herds. Let me lead on softly that the children be able to endure, and I will come unto my lord unto Seir." So, Esau returned to Seir. Jacob settled in Canaan.

Rachel Dies Giving Birth to Her Second Son
Genesis 35: 16-18

They journeyed from Bethel and there went but a little way and Rachel started having hard labor. Her midwife said unto her, "Fear not, thou shalt have this son also." Rachel could not endure. And it came to pass as she was dying, Rachel called his name Benoni (son of pain), but Jacob called him Benjamin.

Jacob's Sons
Genesis 35: 23-26

Leah's Sons

- Reuben: Jacob's first born. He also went in and lay with Bilhah, his father's concubine. Jacob heard about it.

***Because Reuben had laid with Bilhah, he lost his birthright forever. Joseph replaced Reuben.

- Simeon: Second son of Leah and Jacob.

- Levi: He didn't get land because the LORD Himself is his land.

Judah, Issachar, and Zebulun.

Rachel's Sons

   Joseph and Benjamin

Rachel's Handmaiden, Sons of Bilhah

   Dan and Naphtali

Leah's Handmaiden, Sons of Zilpah

   Gad and Asher

*** They are the 12 Tribes of Israel

Remember— Jacob's name was changed to Israel.

Jacob and Esau Bury Their Father, Isaac
Genesis 35: 28-29

Isaac was a hundred and 4 score (180 years old) when he died. Jacob and Esau buried him.

The 12 Tribes of Israel

Joseph and Levi didn't get land. But Joseph had two sons and they inherited Joseph's part. Therefore, making it 12 tribes again.

Jacob Buys Land in Canaan
Genesis 33:17-20

Jacob has settled in Canaan, when he came from Padanaram; and pitched his tent before the city. He bought a parcel of a field where he had spread his tent, at the hand of the children of Hamor, Shechem's father, for a hundred pieces of silver. Jacob erected an altar and called it El-elohe-Israel.

Dinah, Jacob's Daughter Defiled
Genesis 34: 1-12

Dinah, the daughter of Leah, which she bare unto Jacob, went out to see the daughters of the land. When Shechem, the son of Hamor the Hivite, saw her, he took her, laid with her, and defiled her. His soul clave unto Dinah and he loved her, and spake kindly to her. Shechem spoke to his father Hamor, saying, "Get her for me to be my wife." Jacob heard that he had defiled Dinah, his daughter. Now, his sons were with his cattle in the field and Jacob held his peace until they were come. Hamor, the father of Shechem, went out to talk with Jacob. When Jacob's sons came out of the field and heard it, they were grieved and very wroth because he had wrought folly in Israel when he laid with Jacob's daughter, Dinah, which should not have been done. Hamor talked with them saying, "The soul of my son Shechem loves your daughter. I pray you give her him to wife. You make ye marriages with us, and give your daughters unto us, and take our daughters unto you. Ye shall dwell with us and the land shall be before you; dwell and trade ye therein and get you possessions therein." Shechem said unto her father and unto her brothers, "Let me find grace in your eyes, and what ye shall say unto me, I will give. I will give according as ye shall say unto me but give me the damsel to wife."

Brothers to the Rescue
Genesis 34: 13-24

The brothers answered Shechem and Hamor, his father, deceitfully, and said, "Because he has defiled our sister Dinah, we cannot do this thing. To give our sister to one that is uncircumcised, for that were a reproach unto us. But we will consent if you and every male be circumcised. Then we will give our daughters and we will take your daughters to us. But if you will not hearken to us, to be circumcised, then we will take our sister and be gone." Their words pleased Hamor and Shechem, his son. The young man deferred not to do the thing because he had delight in Jacob's daughter: and he was more honorable than all the house of his father. Hamor and Shechem communed with the men of their city. They told them all what was said. Every male was circumcised.

The Brothers Get Revenge
Genesis 34: 25-31

***Look out Hamor and Shechem and all their men!

After the men were circumcised, they were sore and on the third day, two of the sons of Jacob, Simeon and Levi, took each man his sword, and came upon the city and slew Hamor, Shechem, and all the males. They took Dinah out of Shechem's house. The sons of Jacob came upon the slain and spoiled the city because they had defiled their sister. They took their sheep, oxen, and their asses, and that which was in the city, and that which was in the field. And all their wealth, their little ones, their wives they took captive, and spoiled even all that was in the house. Jacob said to Simeon and Levi, "Ye have troubled me to make me to stink among the inhabitants of the land, and being few in number, they shall gather themselves together against me, and slay me; and I shall be destroyed, I and my house." And they said, "Should he deal with our sister as with a harlot?"

Lesson 5

Joseph's Coat of Many Colors
Genesis 37: 1-4

Jacob loved Joseph more than any of his sons. Joseph was 17 years old and was feeding the flock with his brothers. Jacob made him a coat of many colors. When the brothers saw the coat and knew their father loved him more, they hated Joseph and could not speak nicely to him.

Joseph's Dream
Genesis 37: 5-8

Joseph told his brothers that he dreamed they were binding sheaves in the field and his sheaf arose, stood upright, and their sheaves stood around and expressed deep respect (or bowed) to his sheaf. His brothers said, "Shall you indeed rule over us?" And they hated him even more.

Another Dream
Genesis 37: 9-11

"I dreamed another dream. Behold, the sun, moon, and the 11 stars made obeisance to me (respected/bowed down)." He told this to his father, and he said unto Joseph, "Shall I, thy mother, and thy brothers come and bow down to you?"

Israel Sends Joseph to Look for His Brothers
Genesis 37: 12-17

His brothers went to feed the flock. Israel sent Joseph to look for them. "Come back and tell me word of them." A certain man found Joseph wandering in the field and told Joseph he heard his brothers say, "Let us go to Dothan." And he found them there.

The Plot to Get Rid of Joseph
Genesis 37: 18-27

When they saw Joseph from a far off, they conspired to slay him. We will cast him in a pit, and we will say some evil beast hath eaten him and we will see what becomes of his dreams. Reuben (first born) heard it and delivered him out of their hands. "Let us not kill him. Shed no blood but cast him in this pit."

*** Rueben planned to get him out of the pit and take him back to his father.

When Joseph got to his brothers, they stripped his coat off and cast him into the empty pit. They sat down to eat and saw a company of Ishmaelites coming from Gilead with their camels, bearing spices, balm, and myrrh going to Egypt.

***Remember Ishmael, first son of Abraham and Hagar, Sarai's handmaiden she sent into Abram.

Joseph Sold for Twenty Pieces of Silver
Genesis 37: 28-30

His brothers sold Joseph to the Ishmaelites for <u>20 pieces of silver.</u> Reuben returned to the pit and Joseph was gone. He rent (tore off) his clothes. He returned to his brothers and asked, "Where is the child?"

Brothers Lie to Jacob
Genesis 37: 31-35

The brothers killed a kid goat and dipped Joseph's coat in the blood. They brought the coat of many colors to their father and said they found it. They said they don't know if it is Joseph's coat or not. Jacob said, "It is my son's coat. An evil beast hath devoured him. Joseph is without a doubt torn into pieces." Jacob rent, or tore off, his clothes, put on sackcloth, and mourned for his son many days. He refused to let his sons comfort him. He said, "I will go down into the grave unto my son mourning." And he wept for Joseph.

Joseph Heading to Egypt
Genesis 37: 28, 36

Joseph was sold by the Midianites into Egypt to Potiphar, an officer of Pharaoh's, and captain of the guard.

*** Joseph is now a slave.

The Lord is With Joseph
Genesis 39: 1-6

The LORD was with Joseph. He was a prosperous man. He was in the house of his master, the Egyptian. His master saw that the LORD was with him. Joseph found grace in his sight, so he made him overseer over his house and all that he had. The LORD blessed the Egyptian's house for Joseph's sake, and in the field. And Joseph was a goodly person and well favored.

Joseph Refused the Master's Wife
Genesis 39: 7-12

His master's wife cast her eyes upon Joseph. She said, "Lie with me." Joseph refused, and said, "My master has entrusted all that he has to my hand. There is none greater in this house than I. He hasn't kept anything from me but thee, because you are his wife. How can I do this great wickedness and sin against God?" She spake to him day by day and he hearkened not unto her. One day Joseph went into the house to do his business. There was none of the other men in the house. She caught Joseph by the garment saying, "Lie with me." He left his garment in her hand, he fled, and got out.

Wife Lies to Her Husband, Potiphar
Genesis 39: 13-19

When she saw that he left his garment, she called unto the men of the house and said to them, "See this Hebrew that was brought unto us, he came in unto me to lie with me, and I cried with a loud voice. When I cried out, he left his garment with me and fled." She kept the garment until his lord came home. She said, "The Hebrew servant, which thou brought unto us, came in unto me to mock me. When I cried out, he fled." When his master heard what his wife said, his wrath was kindled against Joseph.

*** This is the second time a coat has been used to deceive Joseph!!! Prison for Joseph!!

Butler and Baker Offend Pharaoh
Genesis 40: 1

The Chief Butler and Chief Baker offended their lord. Pharaoh put them in prison, the place where Joseph was.

The Butler and Baker Have Dreams
Genesis 40: 5-8

They each had a dream and when Joseph saw them, they were sad. He asked, "Why do you look so sad?" They said they had a dream and there was no interpreter. Joseph said, "Tell them to me. Do not interpretations belong to God?"

Butler's Dream
Genesis 40: 9-13

"Behold a vine was before me. And in the vine were three branches, and it budded, and her blossoms shot forth; and the clusters brought forth ripe grapes. Pharaoh's cup was in my hand. I took the grapes and pressed them into his cup and gave the cup to him." Joseph said, "The three branches are three days. In three days, Pharaoh will restore you unto thy place and you will be chief butler as before."

"Remember Me," said Joseph.
Genesis 40: 14-15

Remember me and show me kindness. Make mention to Pharaoh and bring me out of this house. For I was stolen away from the land of the Hebrews, and I have done nothing so that I should be in this dungeon.
***Way to go, Butler! Joseph isn't remembered for two years.

Baker's Dream
Genesis 40: 16-19

The baker told Joseph his dream. He said, "I had three white baskets on my head. The uppermost basket had all manner of baked meats for Pharaoh, and the birds came and ate it." Joseph said, "The three baskets are three days. Yet within three days, Pharaoh will lift thy head from off thee, and he shall hang you on a tree; the birds will come and eat thy flesh."

*** Wow, that's not too refreshing!!!

The Dreams Become Reality
Genesis 40:20-23

On the third day was Pharaoh's birthday and he made a feast. He restored the chief butler back to his job and he hanged the baker. The chief butler did not remember Joseph.

Pharaoh's Dreams
Genesis 41: 1-8

Two full years passed, and Pharaoh dreamed. He stood by a river. There came out of the river well-favored kine (cows) feeding in a meadow. And behold, seven other cows came out: ill, lean fleshed, and stood by the others. The ill and skinny cows ate the seven fat cows. Pharaoh awoke. He slept again and dreamed. Behold, seven ears of corn came upon one stalk, rank and good. Then seven thin ears and blasted (withered, blighted, ruined) with the east wind. The thin ears devoured the seven good ears. He awoke. It was a dream. The next morning, his spirit was troubled. He sent for the magician of Egypt and all the wise men, and none could interpret the dream.

The Butler Remembers Joseph
Genesis 41: 9-13

Then the chief butler said, "I do remember when you put me and the chief baker in prison, we both had a dream, and a man interpreted our dream. And both came true. A young Hebrew man."

***Could that be Joseph????

Pharaoh Calls for Joseph
Genesis 41: 14-24

Pharaoh called for Joseph. He shaved and changed raiment and came into Pharaoh. He told Joseph about the dreams, and no one can interpret the dreams. Joseph said, "It is not in me. God shall give the answer." Pharaoh told Joseph the dream.

Pharaoh's Dreams Interpreted by Joseph
Genesis 41: 25-36

"The seven good cows are seven years. The dream is one. The seven thin cows are seven years of famine. Behold, there comes seven years of great plenty throughout all the land of Egypt. And after that, will be seven years of famine, and all the plenty shall be forgotten in the land of Egypt; the famine shall consume the land. It was established by God, and God will shortly bring it to pass. Now, let Pharaoh find a man discreet and wise and set him over the land of Egypt. Let him keep food so that when the seven years of famine come in Egypt, that the land not perish."

Pharaoh Chooses Joseph to Rule
Genesis 41: 37-45

They couldn't find anyone. Pharoah said to Joseph, "God has shown you all this; there is none as discreet and wise as you." So, he was made ruler over all the land of Egypt. Pharaoh called Joseph's name Zaphnathpaaneah; and he gave him a wife, Asenath, the daughter of Potipherah priest of On.

The First Seven Years
Genesis 41: 46-49

Joseph was 30 years old. He went throughout all the land of Egypt. The first seven years, the earth brought up plenty. He laid up the food in the cities, he gathered as the sand of the sea.

Two Sons Born to Joseph
Genesis 41: 50-52

And Joseph had two sons before the famine. He called the first-born Manasseh, for God, hath made me forget my toil and my father's house. The second he called Ephraim, for God hath caused me to be fruitful in the land of my affliction.

The Famine Begins
Genesis 41: 53-57

The seven years of plenty ended. Then there was an inadequate supply of food. People cried to Pharaoh for bread. He told them to go unto Joseph. Famine was over all the face of the earth. Joseph opened up the store house and sold to the Egyptians. And all countries came into Egypt to buy corn.

Joseph's Brothers Go to Egypt
Genesis 42: 1-8

Jacob heard there was corn in Egypt. Joseph's ten brothers went to buy corn. Jacob didn't send Benjamin. Joseph's brothers came and bowed down before him.

***Looks like Joseph's dreams are coming true!!!

Joseph knew them, they didn't know Joseph. "Whence come ye?" They said, "From the land of Canaan to buy food."

Joseph said, "Ye Are Spies."
Genesis 42: 9-17

Joseph said, "Ye are spies." "Nay," they said, "we are true men, not spies. We are 12 brothers, the sons of one man, in the land of Canaan. The youngest stayed with our father and one is not." Joseph said, "It is as I said. You are spies. Hereby ye shall be proved: thou shall not go forth except your youngest brother come hither. Send one of you to get him, and ye shall be kept in prison until I find out the truth." He put them all together into ward three days.

Bring Your Youngest Brother to Me
Genesis 42: 18-24

Joseph said on the third day, "This do and live. One of your brothers will stay here in prison. Go ye, carry corn for the famine to your house. Bring your youngest brother to me, so your words will be verified and ye shall not die." And they did so. Reuben asked Joseph not to sin against the child. They didn't know Joseph understood them because he used an interpreter. Joseph turned from them and wept.

Brothers Depart
Genesis 42: 25-28

Joseph commanded their sacks be filled with corn and give all their money back. Then they departed and one of them opened his sack to feed the ass and he saw the money. He told his brothers, "My money is restored." Their hearts failed them, and they were afraid and said, "What is this God hath done unto us?"

The Brothers Return to Their Father
Genesis 42: 29-35

They told their father all that befell them, and they told him we are to bring our youngest brother to him, then he will know we are not spies. When they emptied their sacks, every man's money was in the sack. They and their father were afraid.

Benjamin Cannot Go To Egypt
Genesis 42: 36-38

He was still grieving for Joseph. Simeon is not here. "You cannot take Benjamin away. If mischief befall him by the way which ye go, then shall ye bring down my gray hairs with sorrow to the grave."

Out of Food, Back to Egypt
Genesis 43: 1-7

Their father Jacob said, "Go again to buy corn."
Judah said, "The man demanded we bring Benjamin, or you will not see my face."
Jacob said, "Why did you tell him about us?"
"We didn't know he would say to bring our brother down."

Judah Will Take Care of Benjamin
Genesis 43: 8-12

Judah said, "Send the lad with me. We will go, that we may live (not starve) and not die, both we, you, and also our little ones. I will be surety for him. If we had not lingered, we would have already been back." Their father Israel said, "It must be so now. Take the man the best fruits in the land in your vessels: a little balm, honey, spices, myrrh, nuts, and almonds. And take double money and give it to him and tell him it was an oversight."

Joseph Sees Benjamin
Genesis 43: 13-17

"Take your brother and go again. And God Almighty give you mercy before this man, that he may send away your other brother and Benjamin. Or I will be bereaved." They took the present, the double money, and Benjamin, rose up, and went to Egypt and stood before Joseph. When Joseph saw Benjamin, he said to the ruler of his house to slay and make ready for these men to dine with him at noon. The man brought the men into Joseph's house.

Brothers to Eat Bread with Joseph
Genesis 43: 18-25

The brothers were afraid. "We came down the first time to buy food. When we left and came to the inn, we opened our sacks, and all the money was in our sacks. We brought it again to you. And other money to buy more food." And Joseph said, "Peace be to you, fear not. Your God and the God of your fathers hath given you treasure in your sacks. I had your money." Then he brought Simeon out to them. The man brought the men into Joseph's house, gave them water to wash their feet. They heard they should eat bread with Joseph.

Joseph's Younger Brother, Benjamin
Genesis 43: 26-30

When Joseph came home, the men brought the presents to him and bowed themselves to the earth. He asked about their father. "Is he yet alive and well?" And they bowed their heads. Joseph said, "Is this your younger brother?" Joseph sought where to weep; and he entered into his chamber and wept there.

Joseph's Meal with His Brothers
Genesis 43: 31-34

Joseph washed his face, refrained himself, and said, "Set on the bread." Joseph sat by himself, his brothers by themselves, and the Egyptians by themselves for it is an abomination for Egyptians to eat bread with Hebrews. They drank and were merry with him.

The Silver Cup
Genesis 44: 1-13

He told the steward of the house to fill the men's sacks with food and to put their money back. And put <u>my silver cup in the sack's mouth of the youngest.</u> As soon as the morning was light, the men were sent away. Before they got far away, Joseph sent his steward to overtake them, and say, "Wherefore have ye rewarded evil for good. <u>You have taken the silver cup."</u> They took all the sacks and checked each one, eldest to the youngest. <u>They found the cup in Benjamin's sack.</u> Then the brothers rent their clothes and returned to the city.

Who Has Joseph's Cup?
Genesis 44: 14-17

Judah came to Joseph and fell before him. Joseph said, "What deed have you done to me?" Judah said, "What shall we say, my lord? What shall we do to clear ourselves?" And Joseph said, "God forbid that I should do so, but whoever is found with the cup shall be my servant. As for you, get up, and peace be to your father."

Judah Begs To Take Benjamin's Place
Genesis 44: 18-34

Judah came near to Joseph, "Let me, I pray thee. You asked about my father and brother, and you wanted to set eyes upon him. And we said that the lad cannot leave his father for if he should, his father would die." Our father said, 'Ye know my wife Rachel bare me two sons. And the one went out from me, and I said that, surely, he is torn in pieces, and I saw him no more. If something happens to Benjamin, I will have sorrow to the grave.' Judah said, "When he sees the lad is not with me, he will die. Let me stay instead of the lad. Let the lad go home."

Joseph Wept Aloud
Genesis 45: 1-8

Joseph could not refrain himself. He cried and told all the men to go out from him. He made himself known to his brothers. He wept aloud. The Egyptians and the house of Pharaoh heard. Joseph said, "I am Joseph; does my father yet live?" His brothers could not answer, they were troubled by his presence. "I am your brother Joseph whom ye sold into Egypt. Do not be grieved or angry at yourselves because God sent me here to preserve life. For two years, famine has been on the land and there are five years left. So now it was not you that sent me, but God. He has made me a father to Pharaoh, lord of all his house, and a ruler throughout all of Egypt."

Tell My Father, Jacob, to Come to Egypt
Genesis 45: 9-15

"Go and tell my father what I have told you. Tell him to come to Egypt, tarry not. Thou shalt dwell in the land of Goshen; you will be near to me, your children, flocks, herds and all thou hast. I will take care of you. Tell my father hither." He fell upon his brother Benjamin's neck and wept, and Benjamin wept. Then he kissed all his brothers and wept.

***This is the beginning of the Israelites being slaves in Egypt.

Pharaoh Tells Joseph to Bring His Father
Genesis 45: 16-20

It pleased Pharaoh. "Go get your father and your household and come unto me. I will give you good land and ye shall eat the fat of the land. Take wagons from Egypt to bring your little ones, your wives, your father, and come dwell here."

Brothers Tell Jacob That Joseph is Alive
Genesis 45: 25-28

When they got to their father, they told him Joseph is alive and governor over all the land of Egypt. Jacob's heart fainted. He didn't believe them. They told him all the words of Joseph and his spirit revived. And Israel said, "Joseph is alive, and I will go see him before I die."

God Tells Jacob to Go See Joseph
Genesis 46: 1-7

And Israel took his journey and came to Beersheba. He offered sacrifices unto the God of his father Isaac. And God spoke to Israel in the visions at night and said, "Jacob, Jacob." And he said, "Here am I." He said, "I am God, the God of your father. Fear not to go to Egypt; for I will make thee a great nation. I will be with you, and your son Joseph shall see you." Jacob rose up and came unto Egypt.

Joseph Sees His Father
Genesis 46: 28-34

He sent Judah to Joseph, and they came to Goshen. Joseph went to meet his father; he fell on his neck and wept a good while. Israel said, "Now let me die, since I have seen thy face and know you are alive." Joseph said, "Now I will take you to Pharaoh and you will meet him."

Pharaoh Meets Jacob and the Brothers
Genesis 47: 1-6

Joseph told Pharaoh, "My father and brothers, flocks, and herds, and all they have come from Canaan. They are in the land of Goshen."
"This is the best land and if thou knowest any men of activity among them, then make them rulers over my cattle," answered Pharaoh.

Jacob Blessed Pharaoh
Genesis 47: 7-12

Joseph brought Jacob his father to Pharaoh and Jacob blessed him. Pharaoh asked, "How old are you?" Jacob replied, "My days of the years are 130 years."

Joseph's Promise to Jacob
Genesis 47: 27-31

Jacob dwelt in the land of Egypt 17 years, they had grown and multiplied. Jacob is now 147 years old. He called to his son Joseph, "I am old and going to die. I pray thee thou put your hand under my thigh; bury me not in Egypt, bury me in the burying place. Sware unto me." Joseph did sware unto him.

Joseph Brings His Sons to Meet Jacob
Genesis 48: 1-7

Joseph heard that his father is sick, and he took his two sons to visit him: Manasseh and Ephraim. Jacob said, "They shall be mine; their grandfather welcomes them."

Jacob Gives His Blessings
Genesis 48: 8-20

Jacob blessed Joseph's sons. His eyes were dim, and he could not see. He brought them near, kissed, and embraced them. "I didn't think I would see you and, lo, God has shown me your seed." He blessed the youngest first and Joseph didn't like that. But Jacob said, "He will be greater. He and his seed shall become a multitude of nations. He said the oldest son will also be great."

Blessing to Jacob's Sons
Genesis 49: 1-28

Jacob called his sons all together to tell them that which shall befall them in the last days. Gather yourselves together, and hear, all you sons of Jacob; and hearken unto Israel your father.

*** Please read verses 3-28 for all the blessings from Jacob.

Jacob Wants to Be Buried With His People
Genesis 49: 29-33

Jacob told his sons, "I am to be buried with my people. Bury me with my fathers in the cave that is in the field of Ephron the Hittite in the land of Canaan which Abraham bought. Buried there is Abraham and Sarah his wife, Isaac and Rebekah his wife, and there I buried Leah." And when Jacob commanded them, he gathered his feet into the bed, gave up the ghost, and died.

Joseph Mourns His Father, Jacob
Genesis 50: 1-3

Joseph fell upon his father's face, wept upon him, and kissed him. Joseph commanded his servants, the physicians, to embalm his father.

Let Me Go Bury My Father
Genesis 50: 4-6

"If I have found grace in your eyes, grant my plea. My father made me swear I would take him back to Canaan to be buried. Now therefore let me go up and bury my father and I will come again." Pharaoh said, "Go and bury your father."

The Brothers Carry Jacob Back to Canaan
Genesis 50: 7-14

Joseph left to bury his father and with him were servants of Pharaoh, elders of his house, and elders of the land of Egypt. All the house of Joseph, his brothers, the little ones, their flocks and herds left Goshen; a very great company. Jacob's sons carried him unto the land of Canaan. Joseph returned to Egypt and all that went with him.

Jacob is Dead and the Brothers Fear Joseph
Genesis 50: 15-18

When the brothers saw that their father was dead, they feared Joseph would hurt them because of what they had done to him. They sent a messenger to Joseph, "Forgive us for what we did to you." And Joseph wept. His brothers fell down before him and said, "Behold, we be thy servants."

Joseph said, "Fear Not."
Genesis 50: 19-21

Joseph said, "Fear not, for am I in the place of God? But as for you, ye thought evil against me; but God meant it to be good, to bring to pass, as it is this day, to save many people. So, fear not. I will take care of you and your little ones." And he comforted them.

Joseph's Death and Burial
Genesis 50:22-26

Joseph dwelt in Egypt, he and his father's house. He lived 110 years. Joseph said to his brothers, "I die. God will surely visit you and bring you out of this land unto the land he swore to Abraham, Isaac, and Jacob." Joseph took an oath of the children of Israel, saying, "<u>God will surely visit you and ye shall carry my bones from hence.</u>" So, Joseph died, they embalmed him, and put him in a coffin in Egypt.

Chapter 3

Lesson 1
God's Land of Promise

Joseph, owner of the coat of many colors has died. He is in a coffin in Egypt.

Joseph Has Died and the Israelites Multiply
Exodus 1: 1-7

Joseph is the top ruler of Egypt, only next to Pharaoh. Jacob, his father, came to Egypt from Canaan with all his household, all of Jacob's brothers. Joseph died, and all his brothers, and all that generation. And all the children of Israel were fruitful and multiplied; the land was filled with them.

The King of Egypt is Worried
Exodus 1: 8-14

Egypt has a new king, and he doesn't know Joseph. The new king said to his people, "The people of Israel are more and mightier than us. Come on. We need to deal wisely with them." He was worried about them joining with other enemies and fighting against them. They set taskmasters (a person who assigns burdensome tasks to others) to afflict them with their burdens. The more they afflicted them, the more they grew. And they were grieved. So, the Egyptians made them serve with rigor. They made their lives bitter with hard bondage. All their service was hard.

The Midwives Fear God
Exodus 1: 15-21

The king told the Hebrew midwives to kill all the male babies and to save the females. The midwives' names are Shiphrah and Puah. They feared God and did not do as the king said. The king called to them and asked, "Why have you done this and saved the men children?" They said unto Pharaoh, "The Hebrew women are not as the Egyptian women." Therefore, God dealt well with the midwives. Because they feared God, He made them houses.

The New King Wants to Get Rid of Hebrew Sons
Exodus: 1: 22

"Every son that is born, cast them into the river, but save the females."

Moses Hidden
Exodus 2: 1-4

Moses was born to a man and woman from the house of Levi. His mother saw he was a goodly child. She hid him three months. When she could no longer hide him, she made an ark of bulrushes, dabbed it with slime and pitch, and put the child in it. She laid it in the reeds by the river's bank. His sister (Miriam) stood afar off to see what would happen to him.

Moses Put in the River
Exodus 2: 5-14

Pharaoh's daughter came to the river to wash herself. She

saw the ark and sent her maid to get it. When she opened it, she saw the Hebrew baby and had compassion on him. Moses' sister said, "Shall I get a Hebrew woman that she may nurse the baby?" Pharaoh's daughter paid Moses' mother to nurse the baby. (Moses' mother was the nurse). The child grew, and his mother brought him to Pharaoh's daughter, and he became her son. She named him Moses because she drew him out of the water. And when Moses was grown, he went out among his brethren and looked at their burdens. He spied an Egyptian hitting a Hebrew. He looked and no one saw him, and he slew the Egyptian and hid him in the sand. When he went out the next day, he saw two Hebrews fighting and he said to him that did the wrong, "Why did you smite thy fellow?" He said, "Who made you a prince and judge? Do you intend to kill me like you killed the Egyptian?" And Moses was afraid, and he said, "Surely this thing is known."

Pharaoh Wants to Kill Moses
Exodus 2: 15-22

When Pharaoh heard what Moses had done, he sought to slay Moses. But Moses had fled to Midian. He sat by a well. Seven daughters of the Priest came to draw water to water their father's flocks. And the shepherds came and drove them away. Moses stood up and helped them water their flocks. When the daughters came to their father, Reuel, he asked, "How did you finish so quickly?" They said, "An Egyptian helped us, and he drew water for the flock." He said, "Call him that he may eat bread." Moses did dwell with the man, and he gave his daughter Zipporah to be his wife, and she bare him a son named Gershom for he said, "I have been a stranger in a strange land."

God Remembers His Covenant
Exodus 2: 23-25

The king of Egypt died, the children of Israel was in bondage, they cried, and God heard their cry. God remembered his covenant with Abraham, Isaac, and Jacob.

Moses Sees the Burning Bush
Exodus 3: 1-9

Moses was keeping his father-in-law's (Jethro) flock. He led them to the backside of the desert and came to the mountain of God, even to Horeb. The angel of the LORD appeared in a flame of fire in a bush. The bush burned but was not consumed. "I will check and see why the bush is not burnt." And when the LORD saw him turn, God called out, "<u>Moses, Moses.</u>" He said, "Here am I." <u>God said, "Don't come any further, take off your shoes, for whereon you stand is Holy Ground. I am the God of your fathers Abraham, Isaac, and Jacob."</u> Moses hid his face because he was afraid to look upon God. God said, "I have seen the affliction of my people, and heard their cry, for I know their sorrows. I have come to deliver them from the Egyptians."

God Will Be With Moses
Exodus 3: 10-18

God said, "I will send you to Pharaoh to bring our people out." Moses said, "Who am I to go?" God said, "I will be with you and when you bring the people out of Egypt, ye shall serve God on the mountain." Moses said, "And when the children of Israel ask who the God of their father is and they ask his name?" And God said, "I AM THAT I AM. You say to them, I AM sent you. Also tell them the LORD God of your fathers, the God of Abraham, Isaac, and Jacob. Now go tell the people that God will bring them out of affliction of the Egyptians. They will be going to a land flowing with milk and honey. You and the elders shall meet with the king of Egypt; tell him to let our people go."

Moses' Rod Turns To a Snake
Exodus 4: 1-5

Moses said they won't believe that the LORD appeared to me. God said, "Throw thy rod on the ground and it will become a snake." He told Moses to get it by the tail and it will turn back to a rod.

Moses Tells God, "I Don't Speak Well."
Exodus 4: 10-13

Moses said, "LORD, I don't speak well. I am slow to speech and slow of tongue." The LORD said, "Who made man's mouth? Now therefore, go and I will be with thy mouth and teach you what to say." And he said, "O my LORD, send, I pray thee, by the hand of him whom thou wilt send."

God Chooses Aaron to Help Moses
Exodus 4: 14-17

The anger of the LORD kindled against Moses. Your brother, Aaron the Levite, can speak well. So, the LORD made Aaron the speaker for the people.

Moses Speaks to His Father-in-law
Exodus 4: 18-20

Moses went to his father-in-law and said, "Let me go and return back to Egypt and see if my brother is still alive." He said, "Go in peace." The LORD said, "Go, return to Egypt, all the men who sought you are dead." Moses took his wife and sons and returned to Egypt. Moses took the rod of God in his hand.

Moses Speaks to Pharaoh
Exodus 4: 21-28

The LORD said to Moses, "When you return to Egypt, see that you do all those wonders before Pharaoh which you have in your hand. But I will harden his heart so that he won't let the people go. You say to Pharaoh, 'Israel is my first-born son. Let my son go, that he may serve me, and if you refuse to let him go, I will slay thy first-born son.'" It came to pass in the inn, that the LORD met him and sought to kill him. Then Zipporah (Moses' wife) took a sharp stone and cut off the foreskin of her son and cast it at his feet and said, "Surely you are a bloody husband to me, because of the circumcision." The LORD told Aaron to go into the wilderness and meet Moses. He went, met him in the Mount of God, and kissed him. Moses told Aaron all the words of the LORD and all the signs he commanded him.

***Moses neglected to get his son circumcised and God wanted to kill him but Zipporah, his wife, saved him. No mention of Moses being circumcised. Moses was probably circumcised at eight days old before he was put into the river at three months old to keep from being killed by the Pharaoh

The Israelites Believe Moses
Exodus 4: 29-31

Moses and Aaron gather the elders together. Aaron spoke the words the LORD had spoken to Moses. The people believed and bowed their heads and worshiped.

Moses and Aaron Visit Pharaoh
Exodus 5: 1-5

Moses and Aaron went in and told Pharaoh, "The LORD God of Israel said, 'Let my people go.'" Pharaoh said, "Who is the LORD that I should obey his voice? I know not the LORD and I will not let Israel go."

The Hebrew People Given More To Do
Exodus 5: 6-14

He commanded the taskmasters, "Don't give the Hebrew people straw to make brick. Let them go and gather straw for themselves. And if their work slacks or they are idle and cry, saying, 'Let us go and sacrifice to our God,' then let more work be laid on them." The taskmasters told the people what Pharaoh said. "Do your work as when you had straw." When the people couldn't do all the work, they were beaten.

Pharaoh is Harsh to the People
Exodus 5: 15-18

The officers of the people cried to Pharaoh, "Why are you so harsh? No straw is given to us to make brick and thy servants are beaten." Pharaoh said, "Ye are idle, and say, 'Let us go and sacrifice to the LORD.' Go now and work, ye shall have no straw, yet you better deliver the tale of bricks."

The People Complain to Moses
Exodus 5: 19-21

The officers saw they were in the midst of evil when Pharaoh said, "You shall not diminish from the bricks of your daily task." They complained to Moses that he had caused Pharaoh to mistreat them.

Moses Prays
Exodus 5: 22-23

Moses prayed to the LORD, "Why have you sent me? Since I came to Pharaoh and spoke your name, he has done evil to this people. You have not delivered the people at all."

God's Renewed Covenant
Exodus 6: 1-8

The LORD said to Moses, "Now you will see what I will do to Pharaoh. For with a strong hand, he will let them go and a strong hand, he will drive them out of his land. I am the LORD. I appeared unto Abraham, Isaac, and Jacob, by the name of God Almighty, but they did not know me by my name JEHOVAH. I also established my covenant with them to give them the land of Canaan. I also have heard the cry of the children of Israel, whom the Egyptians keep in bondage. Tell the children I will bring you out of the burdens of the

Egyptians. And I will, bring you to the land which I did swear to Abraham, Isaac, and Jacob, and I will give it for a heritage: for he said, <u>I AM THE LORD."</u>

<u>The LORD Said to Speak to Pharaoh</u>
Exodus 6: 9-13

Moses spoke to them. They hearkened not because of anguish of spirit and cruel bondage. The LORD said to Moses, "Go speak to Pharaoh to let the children of Israel go out of his land."

<u>Heads of the Fathers of the Levites</u>
Exodus 6: 14-30

These be the heads of their fathers' houses: sons of Levi, sons of Gershon, <u>sons of Merari, and Amram took Jochebed, his father's sister to wife and she bare him Aaron and Moses,</u> sons of Korah, sons of Uzziel, sons of Izhar: These are the heads of the fathers of the Levites. God said, "Bring them out from the land of Egypt." And it came to pass on that day, the LORD spoke to Moses saying, "<u>I AM THE LORD.</u> Speak to Pharaoh all that I say unto you." Moses said, "Behold, I am of uncircumcised lips, and how shall Pharaoh hearken unto me?"

***Please read Exodus 6 for all the Heads of Families in Egypt.

The Egyptians Will Know that I am the LORD
Exodus 7: 1-9

The LORD said to Moses, "See, I have made thee a god to Pharaoh. And Aaron your brother shall be thy prophet. Aaron will tell Pharaoh to let the children of Israel out of his land. I will harden Pharaoh's heart and he will not hearken to you, that I may lay my hand upon Egypt. The Egyptians will know that I am the LORD when I stretch forth my hand upon them and bring my children out." Moses and Aaron did as the LORD commanded. Moses was 80 years old, and Aaron was 83 when they spoke to Pharaoh. The LORD said, "When Pharaoh says, 'Show me a miracle,' say unto Aaron to take thy rod and cast it before Pharaoh and it shall become a serpent."

Aaron's Rod Swallows Their Rods
Exodus 7: 10-13

Aaron cast the rod and it became a serpent. Then Pharaoh called the wise men and the sorcerers (practice black magic). They cast down their rods, and they became serpents. <u>But Aaron's rod swallowed up their rods.</u> God hardened Pharaoh's heart and he hearkened not unto what the LORD had said.

Pharaoh's Instructions
Blood, the First Plague
Exodus 7: 14-25

The LORD said to Moses, "Pharaoh's heart is hardened and he refuses to let the people go. Go to Pharaoh in the morning when he goes to the water and take the rod in thine hand.

And say, 'The LORD God of the Hebrews has sent me to tell you to let my people go, and you wouldn't listen. The LORD said you will know I am the LORD.' I will smite with the rod in my hand the waters which are in the river, and it shall turn to blood. The fish will die, the river will stink, and the Egyptians will not want to drink of the water." The LORD told Moses to tell Aaron, "Take up the rod and stretch out his hand upon the waters of Egypt that they may become blood, and all the water became blood." Pharaoh's heart was hardened, and he did not hearken unto them. The Egyptians dug around and tried to find water to drink but could not find any.

Frogs, the Second Plague
Exodus 8: 1-8

The LORD said, "Go say to Pharaoh, 'Let my people go.' If he refuses, I will smite all the borders with frogs. The frogs will come upon thee, the people, and your servants." Pharaoh refused to let them go. The LORD spoke to Moses, "Tell Aaron to stretch forth the rod and cause frogs to come upon the land of Egypt." The magicians did also.

Pharaoh Burdened
Exodus 8: 8-19

Pharaoh called for Moses, "Take away these frogs and I will let the people go." "Be it known to you that there is none like the LORD our God." Moses asked God to take away the frogs and the frogs died, and the land stank. Again, Pharaoh hardened his heart.

Lice, the Third Plague
Exodus 8: 16-19

The LORD said, "Tell Aaron to stretch out the rod and smite the dust of the land that it may become lice." Aaron did so. The magicians did so also. The magicians said unto Pharaoh, "This is the finger of God." Pharaoh's heart hardened.

Flies, the Fourth Plague
Exodus 8: 20-24

The LORD said to Moses, "When Pharaoh comes to the water in the early morning say, 'Let my people go.' If you do not, I will send swarms of flies upon you, your servants, people in your houses, and also the ground whereon you are. <u>And no swarms of flies will be in the Land of Goshen in which my people dwell.</u> To the end you shall know that God is the LORD in the midst of the earth." God did corrupt the land with flies.

Pharaoh Says Your People Can Go
Exodus 8: 25-32

Pharaoh called for Moses and Aaron. "I will let you go." Moses said, "Let not Pharaoh deal deceitfully anymore in not letting the people go." God removed the flies.
Pharaoh hardened his heart and would not let the people go.

Cattle Die, the Fifth Plague
Exodus: 9: 1-7

God said, "Go tell Pharaoh to let the people go that they may serve me. He will not let them go. The hand of the LORD will be upon the cattle of the land, horses, camels, oxen, asses, and sheep. There shall be very grievous murrain (diseases of cattle, as anthrax). <u>No cattle shall die of the children of Israel.</u> The LORD said tomorrow this will happen; all the cattle of Egypt will die." And Pharaoh's heart was hardened.

Boils, the Sixth Plague
Exodus 9: 8-12

The LORD said to Moses and Aaron, "Take handfuls of ashes from the furnace, and let Moses sprinkle it up toward heaven, and it shall become small dust in the land of Egypt. It shall be a boil breaking forth upon man and beast throughout Egypt." And Moses did as the LORD told him. The magicians could not stand before Moses because of the boils. And the LORD hardened the heart of Pharaoh, and he hearkened not to them.

Warning from Moses
Exodus 9: 22-26

The LORD said to Moses, "Rise up early in the morning and tell Pharaoh, 'Thus saith the LORD God of the Hebrews, let my people go that they may serve me.' I will send all my plagues upon his heart that he may know there is none like me in all the earth, because he will not let my people go. Tomorrow, I will cause it to rain grievous hail, such as not been in Egypt. Gather up thy cattle, all you have in the field, for every man and beast not brought home, the hail shall come down and they will die." The ones that feared the work of the LORD among the servants of Pharaoh brought his servants and cattle into the houses. He that did not regard the LORD's word left his servants and cattle in the field and they will die.

Hail, the Seventh Plague
Exodus 9: 22-26

The LORD told Moses to stretch forth his hand toward heaven, that there would be hail in all the land of Egypt. The LORD sent thunder and hail. There was fire that ran along the ground. The hail and fire mingled together, like none like it in all the land.
<u>Only in the land of Goshen, where the children of Israel were, there was no hail.</u>

Pharaoh Responds to Moses
Exodus 9: 27-35

Pharaoh sent for Moses and Aaron and said, "I have sinned this time. The LORD is righteous. I and my people are wicked. Tell the LORD I will let you go; ye shall stay no longer." Moses said, "As soon as I am gone out of the city, I will spread abroad my hands to the LORD; the thunder and hail will be no more." When Moses left the city, he did as he said. No more thunder and hail. When Pharaoh saw it was over, he sinned again and would not let the people go.

Warning From Moses
Exodus 10: 3-11

Moses and Aaron go again to talk to Pharaoh, but he refused. Moses said, "Because you refused, I will bring locust. They will eat everything; they will fill your houses." Moses turned and went from Pharaoh. Pharaoh's servants asked, "How long shall he be a snare to us? Let the men go that they may serve their God. Do you not know that Egypt is destroyed?" Moses and Aaron were brought again to Pharaoh. He said, "Go and serve your God, but who are they that will go?" Moses said, "We will go with our young and old, all that we have." He said, "Let the LORD be with you. I will let you go."

Locust, the Eighth Plague
Exodus 10: 12-20

The LORD told Moses, "Stretch out your hand over Egypt for the locust. They will eat every herb, even what the hail left." Moses did as the LORD said, and locust was on all the land of Egypt. Then Pharaoh called for Moses and Aaron, and he said, "I have sinned. Forgive me." The LORD turned a mighty strong west wind, which took away all the locusts. But again, the LORD hardened his heart, and he would not let the people go.

Darkness, the Ninth Plague
Exodus 10: 21-26

The LORD told Moses to stretch out his hand toward heaven, that there may be darkness over the land of Egypt. Moses did as the LORD said, and there was a thick darkness. They saw not each other, <u>but the children of Israel had light.</u> Pharaoh called to Moses and said, "Go and serve the LORD. Only let your flocks and herds stay, and your little ones may go." Moses said, "Our cattle must also go with us so we can sacrifice and have burnt offerings. Not one hoof will be left behind."

Pharaoh Warns Moses He Will Die
Exodus 10: 27-29

Pharaoh's heart hardened and he would not let them go. Pharaoh said, "Get away from me. Take heed. If I see your face again, you shall die." Moses said, "You have spoken well. You will not see my face again."

One More Plague for Egypt
Exodus 11: 1

The LORD told Moses, "I will bring one more plague upon Pharaoh and Egypt. Then shall he let the people of Israel go."

Moses Warns of Death of the Firstborn
Exodus 11: 4-10

The LORD told Moses, "About midnight, I will go out into Egypt. All the firstborn in the land of Egypt shall die; from Pharaoh, even of the maidservant, and all the firstborn of the beasts. There shall be a great cry throughout all the land, such as there was none like it, nor shall be again."

*** This was an ultimate disaster, every Egyptian's firstborn died. And the LORD said, "Pharaoh will not hearken to you." The LORD hardened his heart, and he would not let the people go.

The Lamb Shall Be Without Blemish, the Passover
Exodus 12: 1-13

The LORD spoke to Moses and Aaron, "This month shall be the beginning of months. It shall be the first month of the year for you. Tell your people, in the tenth day of this month, every man shall take a lamb for their house. <u>Your lamb shall be without blemish. A male of the first year: a sheep or goat.</u> Keep it up until the 14th of the month: the whole assembly of the congregation of Israel shall kill it in the evening. They will take the blood, strike it on the two side posts and upper door post of the houses wherein then they shall eat it that night. Roast it with fire. Let none of it remain until morning; burn any that is left. Ye shall eat it; with your loins girded, shoes on your feet, staff in your hand, eat it in haste; <u>It is the LORD's Passover.</u> I will pass through Egypt this night and smite all the firstborn in the land of Egypt, both man and beast; and against all the gods of Egypt, I will execute judgment: <u>I am the LORD.</u> The blood I see upon the house's where ye are, <u>I will pass over you, the plague shall not destroy you.</u>"

Passover to Remain a Memorial
Exodus 12: 14-20

This day shall be unto you for a memorial: ye shall keep it a feast to the LORD throughout your generations.

*** They had the Passover feast every year. It was a reminder that Israel was a new nation and had been delivered from Egypt.

Death of the Firstborn, the Tenth Plague
Exodus 12: 29-30

At midnight, the LORD smote all the firstborn in Egypt, of all the people and beasts. And Pharaoh rose up in the night, he and all his servants, and there was a great cry in Egypt, for there was not a house where there was not one dead.

***Pharaoh finally let the Israelite people go.

Lesson 2

God's Promised Land

God's people left the land of Egypt. God led them away through the wilderness to the Red Sea.

***Remember what Joseph made the people of Israel swear ??? This brought tears to my eyes!!!

Bones of Joseph
Exodus 13: 19

And Moses took the bones of Joseph with him <u>for Joseph had straightly sworn the children of Israel, saying, "God will surely visit you; and ye shall carry</u> up my bones away hence with you."

***From what I have read in different notes, the children of Israel were in Egypt 430 years and in captivity 70 years.

<u>Exodus 12:40</u> Now the sojourning of the children of Israel, who dwelt in Egypt, was four hundred and thirty years.

God Leads by a Pillar of Cloud and Fire
Exodus 13: 21-22

The LORD went before them by day in a pillar of a cloud and by night in a pillar of fire to give them light. He didn't take away the pillar.

God Gives the Israelite People Instructions
Exodus 14: 1-4

The LORD spoke to Moses. He had them camping by the sea. Pharaoh will say they are in the wilderness and are shut in. I will harden Pharaoh's heart and he will follow after them; and I will be honored upon Pharaoh, and his host. The Egyptians will know that I am the LORD.

The Israelites Flee , Pharaoh Pursues
Exodus 14: 5-12

It was told to Pharaoh that the people fled, and he and his servants turned against the people. They said, "We have let them go and now they don't serve us." He got his chariot ready. He took 600 chosen chariots and captains over them. His heart was hardened, and he went after the children of Israel. And the Egyptians overtook them camping by the sea.

Israelites Fear the Egyptians
Exodus 14: 10-12

When the children of Israel saw the Egyptians, they were sore afraid. They said to Moses, "Why did you bring us out? To die in the wilderness? Would it not be better to serve the Egyptians than to die in the wilderness?"

The LORD's Salvation
Exodus 14: 13-20

Moses said, "Fear not. Stand still and see the salvation of the LORD which He will show you today. You see the Egyptians today, but you will see them never again. The LORD will fight for you and hold your peace." The LORD told Moses to tell the people to go forward and for Moses to stretch out his rod over the sea, and divide it, and the children of Israel may go on dry ground through the midst of the sea. And the LORD said, "I will harden the hearts of the Egyptians and they will follow you. I will get my honor upon Pharaoh, his host, chariots, and horsemen. And the Egyptians will know that I am the LORD." And the angel of God and the pillar of the cloud moved behind the children of Israel. It was a cloud by day and fire by night so they did not come near.

The Red Sea Parts
Exodus 14: 21-25

Moses stretched out his hand over the sea and the LORD caused the sea to go back by a strong east wind all night. The people went on dry land, the waters were a wall on the right and left. The Egyptians pursued them. In the morning the LORD looked at the Egyptians through the pillar of cloud and fire. He troubled them, he took off the chariot wheels. They said, "Let us flee from them for the LORD fights for them against us."

The LORD Destroys Pharaoh's Army
Exodus 14: 26-31

The LORD said, "Moses, stretch out your hand over the sea that the waters may come upon the Egyptians and their host." Moses did so and the sea returned. The Egyptians fled. The waters covered the chariots and all the host of Pharaoh that came into the sea. <u>The LORD saved Israel that day out of the hand of the Egyptians.</u> And Israel saw that great work which the LORD did upon the Egyptians. The people feared the LORD, and believed the LORD, and his servant Moses.

The Women Sing With Miriam
Exodus 15: 20-22

Miriam, the prophetess, the sister of Aaron and Moses, took a timbrel (tambourine) in her hand and all the other women went out with timbrels and danced, saying, "Sing ye to the LORD, for he hath triumphed gloriously; the horse and his rider he hath thrown in the sea."

***Miriam was the sister of Moses that stood afar off watching out for baby Moses.

The People Grumbled
Exodus 15:23-26

The people grumbled about most everything. The water that was bitter in Marah. They said to Moses, "What shall we drink?" The LORD showed Moses a tree which he cast into the waters and made the waters sweet. Moses said, "If you hearken to the voice of the LORD, he will do what is right in His sight."

They complained that he had brought them into the wilderness and they will starve. The LORD said unto Moses, "I will rain bread (manna) from heaven, and the people can go out and gather it."
And on the sixth day, they shall prepare that which they bring in; it shall be twice as much. Enough for the sabbath.
Exodus 20: 8-10 Remember the sabbath day, to keep it holy. Six days you labor and do your work and rest on the seventh day.

***Jethro, Moses' father-in-law, heard what God had done for the people of Israel. He came and joined them. He also saw that Moses alone was trying to judge the people and handle their problems and needs. He told Moses he will wear away.

Jethro's Wise Advice to Moses
Exodus 18: 17-23

Jethro advised Moses to provide able men that fear God, men of truth, and men that hate covetousness to be rulers over them, to be rulers of thousands, hundreds, fifties and tens. The larger matters, they bring to Moses. Jethro said, "Do this so you can endure."

Moses Called to Mount Sinai by God
Exodus 19: 20-25

The LORD came down to Mount Sinai. He called to Moses, "Come upon the top of the mount." Moses went up. God told Moses to go back down and tell the people and priest not to come on the mount or the LORD himself would break forth upon them. Moses said, "The people can't come up because

Thou chargedst us, to set bounds about the mount and sanctify it. (Holy, set apart)." "Moses, you go down and you and Aaron shall come up." So, Moses spoke to the people.

The Ten Commandments
Exodus 20: 1-17

*** There are 613 laws of Moses and the first ten are the Ten Commandments.

And God spoke all these words, I am the LORD your God, which brought you out of Egypt. God started telling Moses the Commandments. <u>1. Thou shalt have no other gods before me. 2. Thou shall not make any graven image.</u> ** Do not bow down to them, do not serve them. For the LORD thy God am a jealous God. <u>3. Thou shalt not take the name of the LORD thy God in vain.</u> ** The LORD will not hold you guiltless. <u>4. Remember the Sabbath day, to keep it holy.</u> ** Six days labor, 7th day rest. <u>5. Honor thy father and thy mother.</u> ** that thy days may be long upon the land which the LORD thy God giveth thee. <u>6. Thou shalt not kill. 7. Thou shalt not commit adultery. 8. Thou shalt not steal. 9. Thou shalt not bear false witness against thy neighbor. 10. Thou shalt not covet.</u> **Thy neighbor, his house, wife or anything he has.

***The Ten Commandments were revealed to Moses at Mount Sinai and <u>inscribed by the finger of God</u> on two tablets of stone and kept in the Ark of The Covenant.

***God gave Moses the design for the Ark of the Covenant at the foot of Mount Sinai.

***<u>Hebrews 9: 4</u> The Ark contained the golden pot that had manna, Aaron's rod that budded, and the tablets of the Covenant. (Ten Commandments)

*** <u>Revelations 11:19</u> And the temple of God was opened in heaven, and there was seen in His Temple the Ark of his Testament.

God's Instructions for a Tabernacle
Exodus 25: 8-9

God said, "Let them make me a sanctuary, that I may dwell among them." God showed them the pattern so they could make the tabernacle.

The People Melt All Their Gold
Exodus 32

Moses was delayed coming off the mount. They grumbled to Aaron. They gathered all their gold, melted it, and made a golden calf to worship. When Moses saw what they had done, he threw the tablets down and broke them. God told Moses to get thee down for the people have corrupted themselves. When Moses saw them, he took the calf and burnt it in the fire and ground it to powder, and strew it upon the water, and made them drink of it. <u>Exodus 34:</u> The LORD told Moses to hew two more tables of stone like the first and he will write upon them the words that were in the first tablets.

Day of Atonement
Leviticus 16

Yom Kippur is the most important day. It is a yearly holy day. Two goats are offered to God. One is killed and one is driven into the wilderness. The slain goat is presented to God by the priest. This shall be an everlasting statute unto you, to make an atonement for the children of Israel for all their sins once a year.

***As Christians, we have the blessed and purifying hope that Christ died for our sins.

***Jesus Christ died for the sins of the world.

Lesson 3

God's Promised Land
Genesis 15:13

The LORD wrote on the tablets to give the children of Israel the Ten Commandments. God promised Abraham his seed would be a stranger in a land that is not theirs and shall serve them. The Hebrews were in Egypt 430 years. God also told Abraham his descendants would return to the promised land in the fourth generation.

The LORD Commandeth to Keep Manna as a Testimony
Exodus 16: 32-35

Moses said, "This is one thing the LORD commandeth, fill an omer (unit of dry measure) of the manna to be kept for your generations that they may see the bread I have fed you in the wilderness." Moses told Aaron to get a pot and put manna in it. <u>The children of Israel ate manna 40 years</u> until they came to the borders of Canaan.

***The children of Israel complained about most everything. They said in Egypt we ate freely of the cucumbers, melons, leeks, onions, and garlic. But here there is nothing but this manna. (Numbers 11:1-6)

God is Angry with Aaron and Miriam
Numbers 12: 1-12

Moses married an Ethiopian woman and Aaron and Miriam didn't like it. They said, "Hath the LORD only spoken to Moses and not to us." The LORD heard it. (Moses was very meek, above all the men upon the face of the earth.) The LORD spoke suddenly to Moses, Aaron, and Miriam, "Come out here, you three, unto the tabernacle of the congregation." The LORD came down in the pillar of the cloud, stood at the door, and called Aaron and Miriam. God said, "Hear not my words, if there be a prophet among you, I the LORD will make myself known unto him in a vision and will speak unto him in a dream. My servant Moses is not so, who is faithful in all mine house. With him I will speak mouth to mouth, even apparently, and not in dark speeches; and the similitude of the LORD shall he behold. Were you not afraid to speak against my servant Moses?" The anger of the LORD was kindled against them, and he departed. The cloud departed and behold, Miriam became leprous, white as snow. Aaron looked at Miriam and she was leprous. Aaron said to Moses, "Alas, my LORD, I beseech you, lay not the sin upon us. We have done foolishly and have sinned. Let her not be as one dead."

Moses Cried for Miriam to be Healed
Numbers 12: 13-15

Moses cried to the LORD saying, "Heal her now, O God." And the LORD said to Moses, "If her father had but spit in her face, should she not be ashamed seven days? Let her be shut out of the camp seven days, and after that, let her be well again." The people did not journey until Miriam returned to the camp.

Twelve Men Chosen as Spies To Search Canaan
Numbers 13: 1-3

The LORD spoke to Moses, "Send men to search the land of Canaan, which I give to the children of Israel; one from each tribe. All those men were heads of the children of Israel.

Twelve Spies Chosen
Numbers 13: 4-16

One from the tribe of each: Reuben, Simeon, Judah, Issachar, Ephraim, Benjamin, Zebulun, Joseph, Dan, Asher, Naphtali, and Gad.

Spies Sent Out To Survey the Land of Canaan
Numbers 13: 17-20

Moses sent the spies out. "See what the land is like, the people, are they strong or weak, few or many? Is the land good or bad? Are they in tents, or in strong holds. And be ye of good courage and bring some fruit of the land." Now was the time of first-ripe grapes.

Search of the Land for Forty Days
Numbers 13: 21-25

The spies went and searched the land. They came unto Hebron. (Hebron was built seven years before Zoan in Egypt.) They cut off a cluster of grapes, pomegranates and figs. The place was called Eshcol. They returned from searching after 40 days.

Israel Gets Report from the Spies
Numbers 13: 26-30

The spies came to Moses, Aaron, and the congregation and showed them the fruit of the land. It surely does flow with milk and honey. But the people are strong, the cities are walled, and very great. We saw the children of Anak there. The Amalekites are in the south. The Hittites, Jebusites, and Amorites dwell in the mountains and the Canaanites by the sea and by the coast of Jordan. <u>Caleb stilled the people and said, "Let us go up at once and possess it; for we are able to overcome it."</u>

Ten Spies Give a Negative Report
Numbers 13: 31-33

The other men said, "We can't go up against them, they are stronger. The land we searched is a land that eateth up the inhabitants thereof; and all the people are men of great stature. They were like giants, and we are as grasshoppers."

Israelites Murmur Against Moses and Aaron
Numbers 14: 1-5

The congregation cried and wept that night. They murmured against Moses and Aaron. They said, "It would have been better that we had died in Egypt than to die in this wilderness! Let us make a captain and return to Egypt." Moses and Aaron fell on the faces before all the children of Israel.

Joshua and Caleb Declare that the LORD is With Them
Numbers 14: 6-12

Joshua and Caleb, who also went to spy, rent their clothes. They spake to all the company of the children of Israel saying the land is an exceedingly good land. If the LORD delights in us, then He will bring us into this land which floweth with milk and honey. The LORD is with us; fear them not. The congregation bade stone them with stones. The glory of the LORD appeared in the tabernacle of the congregation before all the children of Israel. The LORD said to Moses, "How long wilt this people provoke (anger) me? How long before they believe me for all the signs I have shown them? I will smite them with the pestilence, (fatal epidemic disease, especially bubonic plague) and I will disinherit them."

God Is Angered With Israel
Numbers 14: 13-25

God was angry with the children of Israel and Moses talked to the LORD and asked Him to forgive them. The LORD said, "I have pardoned according to thy word. But as truly as I live, all the earth shall be filled with the glory of the LORD. Because they have seen my glory and my miracles which I did in Egypt and the wilderness, and have tempted me now these ten times, and have not hearkened to my voice, they will not see the land which I sware unto their father, neither shall any of them that provoked me see it. But Caleb had another spirit with him, and hath followed me fully. I will bring him into the land where he went; and his seed shall possess it."

***The only spies that brought back a good report to Moses were Joshua and Caleb. God said because Caleb had a good spirit with him, he will go into the promised land. Also, Joshua was allowed to go in. (Numbers 14:23-24)

Israel is Punished by God
Numbers 14: 26-37

God spoke to Moses and Aaron saying, "How long shall I bear with this evil congregation which murmur against me? Say unto them, 'As truly as I live, ye have spoken in my ears, so will I do to you. You shall die in this wilderness, from 20 years old and older, which have murmured against me. You will not come into the land, only Caleb and Joshua." They will wander in the wilderness 40 years because they didn't believe. No one over 20 will get to go to the promised land.

Miriam's Death and Burial
Numbers 20: 1

The whole congregation came into the desert of Zin in the first month. The people abode in Kadesh. Miriam died and was buried there.

***Moses was not allowed to go into the Promised Land, Canaan, because he did not sanctify (to make holy) God.

The following scripture tells why the LORD didn't allow Moses to go into the Promised Land.

Moses Smote the Rock for Water
Numbers 20: 2-13

There was no water, so the people gathered against Moses and Aaron. "Would God that we had died when our brethren died before the LORD! We and our cattle are going to die here. You brought us out of Egypt to this evil place." Moses and Aaron went from them to the door of the tabernacle and fell upon their faces. The glory of the LORD appeared to them. The LORD told Moses, "Take the rod and gather the people together, and speak unto the rock before their eyes and it shall bring forth water out of the rock." They did gather the people together and he said, "Hear now, ye rebels; must we fetch you water out of the rock?" Moses lifted up his hand and smote the rock twice with his rod; the water came out abundantly. They all drank and also the beasts drank. <u>The LORD spoke to Moses and Aaron, "Because ye believed me not, to sanctify me in the eyes of the children of Israel, you shall not bring this congregation onto the land which I have given them."</u>

Israel is Encouraged
Deuteronomy 31: 1-6

Moses spoke these words to all Israel, "I am 120 years old this day. I can no longer go out and come in. Also, the LORD hath said I shall not go over this Jordan. The LORD will go over before thee, and thou shall possess them. And Joshua shall go before thee. Be strong and of good courage, fear not, nor be afraid of them; for the LORD thy God will go with you. He will not fail thee, nor forsake thee."

Moses Assures Joshua
Deuteronomy 31: 7-8

Moses called to Joshua, "Be strong and of good courage, for thou must go with the people unto the land which the LORD hath sworn unto their fathers, and you shall cause them to inherit it. The LORD will go before thee; He will be with you, he will not fail you, nor forsake you. Fear not, neither be dismayed."

Moses Sees But Cannot Enter the Promised Land
Deuteronomy 34: 1-4

Moses went up on the mountain of Nebo, to the top of Pisgah. The LORD showed him the land which he swore to Abraham, Isaac, and Jacob saying, "I will give it unto thy seed. I have caused thee to see it with your eyes, but you shall never go over thither."

Moses' Death and Burial
Deuteronomy 34: 5-8

So Moses, the servant of the LORD, died there in the land of Moab. God buried Moses in a valley in Moab. No one knows where he was buried. Moses was 120 years old. The children of Israel wept for Moses thirty days.

Joshua To Lead the Children of Israel
Deuteronomy 34: 9

Joshua, the son of Nun, was full of the spirit of wisdom for Moses had laid his hands upon him. And the children of Israel hearkened unto him and did as the LORD commanded Moses.

Moses, the Great Prophet
Deuteronomy 34: 10-12

Never was there a prophet in Israel like unto Moses, whom the LORD knew face to face. In all the signs and wonders of the land of Egypt to Pharaoh.

James 4: 14 What shall be on the morrow? For what is your life? It is even a vapor, that appeareth for a little time, and then vanisheth away.

John 3: 16: For God so loved the world, that he gave his only begotten Son, that whosoever believeth in Him, should not perish but have everlasting life.

Lesson 4

The Promised Land

We learned a few things about the prophet Moses; the LORD knew him face to face. I'll be so glad to meet this amazing man of God. If only we could grasp the knowing and remember, God's spirit is all around us. We can talk to our LORD anytime. He loves us unconditionally. He is with us all the time. Are we sure we do things God is satisfied with? I ask myself this more times than I can count. I am so unworthy.

God Speaks to Joshua
Joshua 1: 1-9

Joshua is now the leader of the children of Israel, after the death of Moses. So now the LORD will speak and deal with Joshua as he did with Moses.

***Joshua means the LORD is Salvation.

The LORD spoke to Joshua and said, "Moses my servant is dead. Now you arise and go over this Jordan, and all this people, and go to the land I give them. Every place you walk on, I have given to you, as I said to Moses. No man shall be able to stand before thee all the days of your life. I will be with you like I was with Moses. Be strong and of good courage. Observe all the law, which Moses commanded thee. The LORD thy God is with thee whithersoever thou goest."

Joshua Sends Men to Spy Out the Land
Joshua 2:1-2

Joshua sent out two men to spy secretly saying, "Go view the land, even Jericho." They went, and they went into the lodge of a harlot's house named Rahab. It was told to the king of Jericho that men came in to search out the country.

Spies Protected by Rahab
Joshua 2: 3-11

The king sent unto Rahab to bring forth the men that came into her. Rahab hid the two spies. "They came into me but I don't know whence they went. It became dark, so maybe they went out the gate." She told them to chase after them. But, she had brought them up to the roof of the house and hid them. As soon as the guards were gone and the gate was shut, Rahab went upon the roof. She said to the men, "I know that the LORD hath given you the land, and your terror is fallen upon us. We have heard how the LORD dried up the water of the Red Sea and brought you out of Egypt. When we heard all this, our hearts did melt, and there was no more courage in any man because of you. For the LORD your God, he is God in heaven above and in the earth."

***Jericho is part of Canaan.

Rahab

She was a harlot of Jericho. She believed that the God of Israel was the true God.

The Spies Trust Rahab
Joshua 2: 12-22

"Now I pray you, swear unto me by the LORD, since I have showed kindness to you that you will show kindness to my father's house and give me a true token that you will save my father, mother, brethren, sister, and all they have, and deliver us from death." They said, "We agree, if you utter not our business." Then she let down a cord through the window, for her house was upon the town wall. She said, "Get to the mountain and hide yourselves there three days, until the pursuers return, then go your way." They said, "Behold, when we come back, thou bind this scarlet thread in the window, bring all your family to your home. And if anyone comes into the street out the doors, his blood shall be upon his head, and we will be guiltless. And whoever is in the house, his blood shall be on our head, if any hand be upon him." She sent them away and she bound the scarlet line in the window. They went to the mountain and stayed three days. The pursuers looked for them but found them not.

Joshua Gets a Report
Joshua 2: 23-24

The spies told Joshua all that befell them and said, "Truly the LORD hath delivered into our hands all the land; they are afraid and do faint because of us."

Joshua 3

Joshua rose early and came to Jordan, he and all the children of Israel, and lodged there before passing over. The ark symbolized the presence of the Holy One of Israel. There was not to be any careless handling of the ark. God was due His proper reverence. Joshua said to the children of Israel, "Come here and hear the words of the LORD your God. Hereby know that the living God is among you, and he will without fail drive out all the Canaanites, Hittites, Hivites, Perizzites, Girgashites, Amorites, and the Jebusites. The ark of the covenant of the LORD will pass over before you into Jordan. Take 12 men out of the tribes of Israel. As soon as the soles of the feet of the priest that bear the ark of the LORD, the waters of Jordan shall rest. Jordan shall be cut off from the waters that come down from above; and they shall stand upon a heap." The people passed over on dry ground in the midst of the Jordan, until they passed through.

***The people passed over on dry ground. God, and all his power, stopped the Red Sea and now the Jordan River. We serve an amazing God.

The Twelve Stones Become a Memorial
Joshua 4: 1-9

The LORD spoke to Joshua and told him to tell the 12 men of every tribe to take twelve stones and carry them and leave them where you lodge tonight. This may be a sign among you, that when your children ask, "What mean ye by these stones?" Ye answer, "The waters of the Jordan were cut off before the ark of the covenant of the LORD when it passed over Jordan." These stones shall be a memorial unto the children of Israel forever.

The Assault of Jericho and Their Fall
Joshua 6: 1-10

Jericho was shut up because of the children of Israel. The LORD said to Joshua, "See, I have given into thine hand Jericho. Ye shall encompass the city, all ye men of war, and go around the city once. Do it for 6 days. And seven priests shall bear before the ark 7 trumpets of ram's horns. And the 7th day, ye shall encompass the city 7 times, and the priests shall blow their trumpets and when the people hear the sound of the trumpet, all the people will shout with a great shout, and the wall of the city shall fall down flat, and the people shall ascend (rise) up every man straight before him." Joshua told the people, "Do not shout, nor make any noise, no word shall come out of your mouth, until the day I tell you to shout."

***All this fell into place as the LORD told them.

The Spies Bring Rahab and Her Family to Safety
Joshua 6:22-23

Joshua said to the two men that had spied out the country, "Go to the harlot's house, bring her out, and all that she hath." So, they brought out Rahab's father and all the family.

The Destruction of Jericho
Joshua 6: 24-27

They burned the city with fire, and all that was there. They saved the silver and gold, vessels of brass and iron, and they put it in the treasury of the house of the LORD. The LORD was with Joshua; and his fame was heard throughout all the country.

Land Divided
Joshua 13

They divided all the land between the tribes, except for the Levites.

The LORD God is Levi's Inheritance
Joshua 13:33

But unto the tribe of Levi, Moses gave not any inheritance. "The LORD God of Israel was their inheritance," as he said unto them.

Israel Hears What Joshua Has to Say
Joshua 23: 1-5

And it came to pass, Joshua called for all Israel, elders, their heads, judges, and their officers and told them, "I am old and stricken in age. Ye have seen all that the LORD your God has done for you; He has fought for you."

Do Not Turn From God
Joshua 23: 6 - 8

Joshua reminded them of all the LORD had done for them and to always do the right thing. "Do not turn aside therefrom to the right hand or to the left. Cleave unto the LORD your God, as ye have done to this day."

Joshua's Death and Burial
Joshua 24: 29-31

And it came to pass, Joshua the son of Nun, the servant of the LORD, died. He was 110 years old. They buried him in the border of his inheritance.

Bones of Joseph
Joshua 24: 32-33

They buried the bones of Joseph which the children of Israel brought from Egypt. He was buried in Shechem, in a parcel of ground which Jacob bought from the sons of Hamor, the father of Shechem, for a hundred pieces of silver; and it became the inheritance of the children of Joseph.

***It is so amazing to me that over 400 years, the children of Israel remembered to bring the bones of Joseph out of Egypt. A promise kept!!!

Lesson 5

Joshua Speaks to the Children of Israel
Joshua 3: 9-10

Joshua said to the children of Israel, "Come hither, and hear the words of the LORD your God. Hereby ye shall know that the living God is about you and that he will without fail drive out from before you the Canaanites, the Hittites, the Hivites, the Perizzites, the Girgashites, the Amorites, and the Jebusites.

***They must all be completely wiped out. These people are bad and would lead the people astray! (Joshua 10:20-21)

An Angel Rebuked Israel
Judges 2: 1-5

And the angel of the LORD said, "I have made you to go up out of Egypt and brought you to the land I swore unto your fathers, and I said I will never break my covenant with you. You shall make no league (no covenant or compact between you and them). Ye shall throw down their altars. But ye have not obeyed my voice. Why have ye done this? They shall be as thorns in your sides, and their gods shall be a snare to you." It came to pass when the angel of the LORD spoke these words to the children of Israel, they lifted up their voice and wept.

The People Serve the LORD
Judges 2: 6-7

Joshua let the people go unto his inheritance to possess the land. The people served the LORD all the days of Joshua and all the elders that out lived Joshua. The ones that had seen all the great works of the LORD.

Joshua's Death and Burial
Judges 2: 8-10

Joshua, the son of Nun, the servant of the LORD died. He was 110 years old. They buried him in the border of his inheritance. And there arose another generation which did not know the LORD, nor all the works which the LORD had done for Israel.

God Is Angered Toward Israel
Judges 2: 11-15

The children of Israel did evil in the sight of the LORD. They served Baal. They forsook the God of their fathers; they followed other gods. The anger of the LORD was hot against them. He delivered them into the hands of spoilers that spoiled them, and sold them into the hands of their enemies, so that they could no longer stand before their enemies. Everywhere they went the hand of the LORD was against them for evil.

***They wouldn't listen. We are like that at times. We plan or say we are going to do better and then we find ourselves back in the same old ways of sin. We know better, we just don't do better, or we have someone or something to help us get back on the same old sinful track.

***Moses had warned the children of Israel to destroy the Canaanites, Hittites, Hivites, and the Jebusites. But what did they do? Did they listen?

God is Forgotten
Judges 3: 6-7

They took their daughters to be their wives and gave their daughters to their sons and served their gods. They forgot the LORD their God.

***The LORD was not pleased with the children of Israel. They did evil. So therefore, because of their evil ways, many trials and tribulations came to them.

Israel Delivered Seven Years to the Midianites
Judges 6: 1-10

The children of Israel did evil in the sight of the LORD and the LORD delivered them unto the hand of the Midian seven years. They were mistreated and came up against them. It came to pass, and they cried out to the LORD. The LORD said, "I brought you up from Egypt out of bondage. Out of the hand of the Egyptians and gave you the land. I said unto you, 'I am the LORD your God,' but ye have not obeyed my voice."

Gideon

Gideon was from a poor family. He was the youngest but he was a mighty man of war. God sent an angel to tell him the LORD is with him. He was called to judge and save the Israelites after they sinned. Gideon was a faithful ruler.

Gideon Sees an Angel of the LORD
Judges 6: 11-13

An angel of the LORD came, and he sat under an oak. Gideon and his father threshed wheat by the wine press to hide from the Midianites. The angel of the LORD appeared to Gideon and said, "The LORD is with thee thou mighty man of valor (courage or bravery)." Gideon said, "My LORD, if you be with us, then why is all this befallen us? Where are all the miracles our fathers told us? Did not the LORD bring us up from Egypt? But now the LORD hath forsaken us and delivered us into the hands of the Midianites."

Israel is Saved by Gideon
Judges 6: 14-21

And the LORD said, "Go in this thy might, and thou shalt save Israel from the Midianites. Have not I sent thee?" And he said, "Oh my LORD, wherewith shall I save Israel? My family is poor, and I am the least in my father's house." The LORD told him he will be with him. He said, "If I have found grace in thy sight, show me a sign that thou talkest with me." Gideon went in and made ready a kid and unleavened cakes. The flesh he put in a basket and the broth in a pot and brought it out unto him under the oak and presented it. The angel of the LORD said, "Take the flesh and unleavened cakes and lay them on this rock and pour out the broth." And he did so. Then the angel of the LORD put forth the end of the staff, touched the flesh and unleavened cakes, and there arose a fire out of the rock and consumed the flesh and cakes. Then the angel of the LORD departed out of his sight.

Gideon Calls the Altar Jehovah-Shalom
Judges 6: 22-27

Gideon feared death because he had <u>seen an angel of the LORD face to face.</u> And the LORD said unto him, "Peace be unto thee; fear not, thou shalt not die." Then Gideon built an altar there unto the LORD and called it Jehovah-Shalom. And that night the LORD told him to take thy father's young bullock, even the second bullock of seven years old, and throw down the altar of Baal that thy father hath and cut down the grove that is by it. And build an altar unto the LORD thy God upon the top of this rock, in the ordered place, and take the second bullock and offer a burnt sacrifice. Then Gideon took 10 men of his servants and did as the LORD said. Because he feared his father's household and the men of the city, he did it by night, not by day.

The Men Want to Kill Gideon
Judges 6: 28-32

When the men rose up, the altar of Baal was gone. They said, "Who hath done this thing?" The men said to Joash, "Bring out your son, that he may die." God did deliver them into Gideon's hands. God told him his army was too large.

God's Way of Selecting an Army
Judges 7: 4-8

The LORD said to Gideon, "The people are yet too many. Bring them down unto the water, and it shall be that of whom I say unto thee, 'This shall go with thee,' and of whomever I say unto thee, 'This shall not go with thee.' So he brought the people down to the water. And the LORD said, "Everyone that lappeth the water with his tongue, as a dog, set them by himself; likewise, everyone that boweth down upon his knees to drink." And the number that lapped, putting their hand to their mouth, were 300 men, but all the rest of the people bowed down on their knees. The LORD said, "300 men that lapped will I save you." So, the people took victuals (food or provisions) in their hands, and their trumpets.

Gideon Gives the Men Their Weapons
Judges 7: 15-23

Gideon divided the 300 men unto three companies, put a trumpet in every man's hand, with empty pitchers, and lamps within the pitchers. He told the men to do as he does when I come to the outside of the camp. "When I blow a trumpet, I and all that are with me, then blow your trumpets on every side of the camp, and say, 'The Sword of the LORD, and of Gideon.'" They came unto the camp, blew the trumpets, and brake the pitchers that were in their hands. They stood around the camp and all the host ran, cried, and fled. And the men of Israel gathered themselves together out of Naphtali, and out of Asher, and Manasseh, and pursued the Midianites.

Gideon, a Faithful Ruler
Judges 8: 22-37

The men of Israel said unto Gideon, rule over us, both thou and thy son, and thy son's son also for thou has delivered us from the land of Midian. Gideon said, "I will not rule over you and neither my son. The LORD shall rule over you." The country was in quietness 40 years in the days of Gideon.

Gideon's Death and Burial
Judges 8: 32

Gideon, the son of Joash, died in a good old age and was buried in the sepulcher of Joash his father.

Israel Did Evil Things
Judges 13: 1-7

The children of Israel did evil in the sight of the LORD; and the LORD delivered them into the hand of the Philistines 40 years. There was a man of Zorah whose name was Manoah; and his wife was barren. An angel of the LORD appeared to her and said, "You will conceive and bear a son. So beware, do not drink wine nor strong drink, eat not any unclean thing. You will bear a son; and no razor shall come on his head for he shall be a Nazarite unto God from the womb: and he shall begin to deliver Israel out of the hand of the Philistines." And the woman told her husband and said a man of God came to me and his countenance was like the countenance of an angel of God, very terrible. He did not tell me his name. But he said unto me, Behold, thou shalt conceive, and bear a son; and now drink no wine nor strong drink, neither eat any unclean thing: for the child shall be a Nazarite to God from the womb to the day of his death.

Manoah's Request to the LORD
Judges 13: 8-14

Manoah asked the LORD to come again and teach them concerning the child. God did hearken to his voice; the angel of the LORD God came again to the woman, but Manoah was not with her. She ran and told her husband he was there. Manoah arose and went after his wife, and asked the man, "Art thou the man that spoke to the woman?" He said, "I am." Manoah said, "How shall we order the child, and how shall we do unto him?" The angel of the LORD said unto Manoah, "Of all that I said unto the woman, let her beware."

Manoah's Burnt Offering
Judges 13: 15-21

Manoah said to the angel, "Let us make ready a kid for thee." The angel of the LORD said, "Though thou detain me, I will not eat. If thou wilt offer a burnt offering, you must offer it to the LORD." For Manoah did not know he was an angel of the LORD. Manoah asked, "What is your name, that we may honor thee when your sayings come to pass?" The angel said, "My name is a secret. Why ask my name?" So Manoah took a kid and offered it upon the rock unto the LORD. When the flame went up toward heaven from off the altar, the angel of the LORD ascended in the flame.

Manoah and His Wife Believe They Will Die
Judges 13:22-23

Manoah and his wife looked on and fell on their faces to the ground. The angel of the LORD did not appear to them again. Manoah said to his wife, "We shall surely die because we have seen God." His wife said, "If the LORD were pleased to kill us, He would not have received a burnt offering or showed us all these things or told us such things."

***Isn't it funny how God uses a woman to keep things straight?

Samson's Birth
Judges 13: 24-25

The woman bare a son and called his name Samson. He grew and the LORD blessed him. The spirit of the LORD began to move him at times.

Doings of Samson
Judges 14

***Samson saw a woman in Timnath of the daughters of the Philistines. He told his parents, "Get her for me to wife." They said, "Can you not get a wife from your own brethren?" Samson said, "Get her for me." But his parents knew not that it was of the LORD, for at that time the Philistines had dominion over Israel.

***As he and his parents go to Timnath, a young lion roared against him and he killed it.

***He went down and talked to the woman. She pleased

Samson well. After a time, he returned to take her. He saw the carcass of a lion with a swarm of bees and honey in the carcass. He took some in his hands and went on eating. He gave also to his parents to eat. He didn't tell them about killing the lion or that he took the honey from a lion carcass.

Continue Reading About Samson
Judges 14 and 15

This is for your own information about the mighty Samson.

Samson Displays His Strength
Judges 16: 1-3

Samson went to Gaza and saw a harlot and went into her. When it was told to the Gazites, they gathered around and laid wait for him saying they will kill him in the morning. Samson lay till midnight and arose. He took the doors and two posts of the gate of the city and went away with them on his shoulders and carried them to the top of a hill that is before Hebron.

Delilah Betrays Samson
Judges 16: 4-14

It came to pass that he loved a woman whose name was Delilah. The Philistines came to her and said, "Entice him and find out wherein his great strength is. And we will give thee, every one of us, eleven hundred pieces of silver. Delilah said to Samson, "Tell me wherein your strength is." Samson said, "If they bind me with seven green withs that were never dried, then I shall be weak like any other man." So the men did this and he broke them. So his strength was not known. And Delilah said, "You have mocked me and lied. Now tell me wherewith thou mighest be bound." He said, "If they bind me with new ropes, never used, then I shall be weak." They did bind him and he broke them like a thread. Delilah said, "You have mocked me and told me lies. Tell me wherewith thou might be bound." He said, "If thou weavest the seven locks of my head with the loom." And she fastened it with a pin. She said, "The Philistines be upon you, Samson." And he walked away.

Samson's Strength is Finally Revealed
Judges 16: 15-22

She said, "How can you say you love me when your heart is not with me? You have mocked me three times." It came to pass, she pressed him daily and urged him so that his soul was vexed (irritated; annoyed) unto death. He told her all his heart. "There hath not come a razor upon my head; for I have been a Nazarite unto God from my mother's womb. If shaven, my strength will go from me." So she sent and told the Philistines. She made him to sleep upon her knees after they gave her the money. And she called a man to shave off the seven locks of his head, and his strength went from him. Samson awoke and said, "I will go out as other times and shake myself." And he wist not that the LORD was departed from him. The Philistines took and put out his eyes, brought him down to Gaza, and bound him with fetters of brass. He did grind in the prison house. The hair of his head began to grow again.

The Philistines' Make Sport of Samson
Judges 16: 23-27

The lords of the Philistines gathered together to offer a great sacrifice to Dagon their god and rejoice for their god delivered Samson, our enemy into our hand. So they praised their god. It came to pass, when their hearts were merry, they said, "Call for Samson." And they made them a sport and they set him between the pillars.

Samson Talking to the Lad
Judges 16: 26-27

Samson said unto the lad that held him by the hand, "Suffer me that I may feel the pillars where the house stands, that I may lean upon them." The house was full of men and women; and all the lords of the Philistines were there. On the roof was about 3000 men and women that beheld while Samson was sport.

Samson Prays to God
Judges 16: 28-29

Samson prayed, "O LORD God, remember me, I pray thee. Strengthen me, I pray thee, only this once, O God, that I may be at once avenged of the Philistines for my two eyes." And he took hold of the pillars upon which the house stood, one in his right hand and one in his left hand.

Samson's Death and Burial
Judges 16: 30-31

He said, "Let me die with the Philistines." And he bowed himself with all his might, the house fell upon all the people. It killed large numbers instantly. It wiped out all the key Philistine leadership. Then his brethren and all the house of his father came and took him, they buried him between Zorah and Eshtaol in the burying place of Manoah.

***Samson finally performed a selfless act.

Elkanah and His Two Wives
I Samuel 1: 1-8

There was a man named Elkanah and he had two wives, Hannah and she had no children, and Peninnah and she had children. He went out of his city to worship and sacrifice unto the LORD of Hosts. And the two sons of Eli, Hophni and Phinehas, the priests of the LORD were there. Elkanah offered portions to Peninnah, and to all her sons and daughters. But to Hannah he gave a worthy portion; for he loved Hannah. But the LORD had shut up her womb. When she went up to the house of the LORD, she did not eat, she wept. Elkanah said, "Hannah, why weepest thou? Why is thy heart grieved? Am I not better to you than 10 sons?"

Eli Watches Hannah Pray
I Samuel 1: 9-18

Hannah rose up after they had eaten. Now Eli the priest sat on a seat by a post of the temple of the LORD. She was in bitterness of soul, she prayed unto the LORD, and wept sore. She vowed a vow and said, "O LORD of hosts, if thou will give me a son, I will give him unto the LORD all the days of his life and there shall no razor come upon his head." And it came to pass, as she continued to pray, that Eli marked (noticed) her mouth. She spoke from her heart, only her lips moved, but her voice was not heard. Eli thought she was drunk. Eli said, "How long wilt thou be drunken? Put away your wine." She said, "No, my lord, I am a woman of sorrowful spirit. I have not drunk wine or strong drink. I have poured out my soul to the LORD." Then Eli said, "Go in peace and God of Israel grant thee thy petition that you have asked." So she went her way, and did eat, and her countenance was no more sad.

Birth of Samuel
I Samuel 1: 19-23

Elkanah knew his wife Hannah, and the LORD remembered her. She conceived, and bare a son and called his name Samuel, saying, "Because I have asked him of the LORD." Her husband Elkanah and his house went up to offer unto the LORD the yearly sacrifice. But Hannah did not go. She said, "I will go when the child is weaned, and then I will bring him, that he may appear before the LORD, and there abide forever."

Hannah Brings Samuel to Eli
I Samuel 1: 24-28

When Hannah weaned him, she took him up with her, with three bullocks, flour, bottle of wine, and brought him unto the house of the LORD in Shiloh. The child was young. She brought the child to Eli and told him she was the woman that stood by him praying unto the LORD. I have lent him to the LORD as long as he lives.

***Samuel first heard God calling him when he lived with Eli. He thought it was Eli calling him. God called him to be a Hebrew prophet. Samuel was the last judge of Israel.

Samuel Hears the LORD's Call
I Samuel 3: 1-9

Samuel ministered unto the LORD before Eli. It came to pass when Eli laid down in his place, his eyes dim, he could not see. And Samuel laid down to sleep. The LORD called Samuel and he answered, "Here am I." He ran to Eli and said, "Here am I; for you called me." Eli said, "I called you not; lie down again." He went and laid down. The LORD called again, "Samuel." He went to Eli again and said, "Here am I, for you did call." Eli said, "I called not, my son; lie down again." Now Samuel did not yet know the LORD, neither was the word of the LORD yet revealed to him. And the LORD called Samuel the third time. He arose and went to Eli, "Here am I; for you did call me." And Eli realized that the LORD had called the child. Eli said, "Go lay down and it shall be if you are called say, "Speak LORD; for thy servant heareth." Samuel laid down.

God Called to Samuel
I Samuel 3: 10-18

The LORD came, and stood, and called, "Samuel, Samuel." Samuel said, "Speak; for thy servant heareth." The LORD said to Samuel, "I will perform against Eli all things I have spoken concerning his house. When I begin, I will also make an end.

I have told him I will judge his house forever which he knoweth because his sons made themselves vile, and he restrained them not. I have sworn to the house of Eli that the iniquity of Eli's house shall not be purged with sacrifice nor offering forever." Samuel lay until morning. He feared to tell Eli the vision. Eli said, "What is this thing the LORD hath said to you? Hide nothing from me." Samuel told him all and hid nothing.

Samuel Becomes a Prophet
I Samuel 3: 19-21

Samuel grew and the LORD was with him and did not let none of his words fall to the ground. And all Israel, from Dan to Beersheba, knew that Samuel was to be a prophet of the LORD. The LORD appeared again in Shiloh for the LORD revealed himself to Samuel by the word of the LORD.

Israel Versus the Philistines
I Samuel 4: 1-2

Israel went out against the Philistines. Israel was smitten (struck) by the Philistines. They slew the army in the field, about 4000 men.

Philistines Capture the Ark
I Samuel 4: 3-9

The elders said, "Wherefore hath the LORD smitten us today before the Philistines? Let us fetch the ark of the covenant of the LORD out of Shiloh unto us, that it may save us from our enemies." The people went to get the ark. When the ark of the covenant of the LORD came into the camp, all Israel shouted with a great shout. When the Philistines heard the noise, they said, "What meaneth the noise of this great shout in the camp of the Hebrews?" And they understood that the ark of the LORD was in the camp. They were afraid. They said, "God is come to their camp. Woe unto us! Who shall deliver us out of the hand of this mighty God? For it is the God that smote the Egyptians with all the plagues." Be strong and quiet yourselves like men, O ye Philistines, that ye may be servants of the Hebrews. Quiet yourselves like men, and fight.

Israel Loses the Ark in Battle
I Samuel 4: 10-17

The Philistines fought and Israel was smitten. There fell 30,000 footmen. The Ark of God was taken. The two sons of Eli were slain. A man of Benjamin ran out of the army. He came to Shiloh the same day and rent his clothes. Eli sat upon a seat by the wayside watching for his heart trembled for the ark of God. When the man told that the ark had been captured, all the city cried out. Eli said, "What is all the noise?" The man told Eli. Now Eli was 98 years old and he could not see. "Israel fled before the Philistines, and your two sons are dead and the ark of God is taken."

Eli's Death
I Samuel 4: 18

When he said the Ark of God is taken, Eli fell from his seat backward by the side of the gate and broke his neck and died. He had judged Israel for 40 years.

Israel Rejects God
I Samuel 8

Samuel tries to make the people understand that if man rules over them, it might not be a good thing. He said, "God is King." The LORD said unto Samuel, "Hearken unto the voice of the people in all that they say for they have not rejected you, but they have rejected Me, that I should not reign over them. They have forsaken Me and served other gods."

Read the book of Ruth.
It is a short book with a lot of good Information.

***Boaz did marry Ruth.

***Rahab was the harlot at Jericho, the mother of Boaz.

Chapter 4

Lesson 1

Well, we have met many men and women of God. The Israelite's have left Egypt from bondage and found the promised land that God promised Abraham, Isaac, and Jacob. So far in my study of God's Word, the one person I want to meet in heaven after I see Jesus, and my family— especially my sweet, precious momma— is Moses. God wants us to worship only Him. Monotheistic is believing in only one true God. Polytheistic is the worship of many gods. The Canaanites worshiped many gods. Samuel tried to explain to the Israelite's that a king to judge them would take their sons to work for him as horsemen and run his chariots and their daughters will be made to cook or bake. He will take a 10th of your seed. Ye will cry out in that day because of your king which ye shall have chosen, and the LORD will not hear you in that day.

Saul, Son of Kish, to Become King
I Samuel 9: 1-11

There was a man from the tribe of Benjamin, whose name was Kish, and he had a son named Saul, a choice young man, goodly. He was handsome and tall. The asses of Kish, Saul's father, were lost. Saul and his servant searched for them but did not find them. Saul said, "Come, let us return lest my father look for us." The servant said, "Behold now, in this city is a man of God. He is an honorable man. All that he says comes to pass. Now let us go thither. He can show us the way we should go." Saul said, "But what shall we bring the man? We have no present to take him." The servant said, "I have here part of a shekel of silver I will give to the man of God to tell us our way." So Saul said, "Come, let us go." So they went unto the city where the man of God was. Some maidens were out to draw water. They told Saul and the servant where they could find the Seer, which is what a prophet was called at that time. A Seer is a person who prophesies future events. He has spiritual insight of knowledge.

The Meeting of Samuel and Saul
I Samuel 9: 14-19

The LORD had told Samuel in his ear the day before Saul came saying, "Tomorrow about this time, I will send a man out of the land of Benjamin, and thou shalt anoint him to be captain over my people, Israel, that he may save my people out of the hand of the Philistine. For I have looked upon my people because their cry is come unto me." Saul asked, "Where is the Seer's house." Samuel said, "I am the Seer. Go up before me to the high places, for ye shall eat with me today. Tomorrow I will tell you all that is in your heart."

Samuel Anoints Saul
I Samuel 10: 1

Samuel took a vial of oil and poured it upon Saul's head and kissed him. He said, "Is it not because the LORD hath anointed thee to be captain over his inheritance?"

Saul Gets Instructions from Samuel
I Samuel 10: 2-8

"When you depart from me, you will find two men by Rachel's sepulcher, and they will tell you the asses you went to seek are found. Your father hath left care of them for you saying, 'What shall I do for my son?' Then you will go on forward and come to the plain of Tabor, and you will meet three men going up to God to Bethel, one carrying three kids, one carrying three loaves of bread, the other carrying a bottle of wine. They will salute you, and give you two loaves of bread, which you will receive. After that, you will come to the hill of God, where it is the garrison (body of troops) of the Philistines. And it shall come to pass, when you come into the city, you will meet a company of prophets coming down from the high place with a psaltery, tabret (like a small drum), and a pipe harp and they shall prophesy. And the Spirit of the LORD will come to you and you will prophesy with them and shall be turned into another man. For God is with thee. And you shall go down before me to Gilgal, and I will come down to you to offer burnt offerings and to sacrifice peace offerings. Seven days you will tarry, till I come to you and show you what to do."

God Gives Saul Another Heart
I Samuel 10: 9

And when Saul turned his back to go to Samuel, God gave him another heart. And all these signs came to pass that day. He met with the prophets and they prophesied there.

***Saul started his ministry in greatness. As time passed, he rebelled against God's word. He trusted his own self more than God. Saul's son Jonathan is the one man that declared war on the Philistines. But Saul took all the credit when he blew his trumpet to rally all the people.

***Have you ever had a friend like that? How does/did it make you feel??? The Spirit of The LORD came powerfully upon Saul. God changed him into a different person. Samuel had agreed to come and offer sacrifices to seek God's favor on Israel's army. But when he didn't arrive at the appointed time, Saul's army was so intimidated by their enemies that the soldiers began to desert. Saul decided to offer sacrifices himself.

The End for Saul's Kingdom
I Samuel 13: 13-14

Samuel said to Saul, "You have done foolishly; you have not kept the Commandments of the LORD thy God. The LORD would have established thy kingdom upon Israel forever. But now thy kingdom shall not continue. The LORD has sought a man after his own heart. He will be captain over his people because you have not kept that which the LORD commanded you."

***WOW!!! A man after God's own heart! Could this be David?

I Samuel 14

Jonathan was the true leader of Israel. Saul trusted his own army. Jonathan trusted God.

I Samuel 15

Saul stopped trusting God. He began to trust himself. He started blaming others. He lost his friend Samuel, the man that tried to teach him right before the LORD. God rejected Saul because he was proud. Saul failed God and God was not happy with him.

Saul's Sin, God Rejects Him
I Samuel 15: 26-31

Samuel told Saul, "The LORD has rejected you from being king over Israel. The LORD hath rent the kingdom of Israel from you this day, and hath given it to a neighbor, that is better than you." Saul said, "I have sinned; yet honor me now, I pray thee, before the elders of my people, and before Israel, and turn again with me, that I may worship the LORD thy God." Samuel turned and Saul worshiped the LORD.

Jonathan, Saul's Son

Saul was very destructive, believing only in himself and not following the LORD's commandments. Jonathan was a follower and believer of God. Because of Saul's behavior, God removed kingship from Saul's family.

Saul Should Have Killed Agag
I Samuel 15: 32-35

Saul did not kill Agag, the king of Amalekites. He allowed the people to keep the sheep and cattle, all that was good. Samuel said, "Bring Agag to me." Agag came to him delicately, and said, "Surely the bitterness of death is past." Samuel said, "As thy sword has made women childless, so shall your mother be childless." And Samuel hewed (to strike forcibly with a sword, ax, to chop, or hack) Agag in pieces. Samuel came to see Saul no more. Until the day of his death, he did mourn for Saul. And the LORD repented that He had made Saul king over Israel.

Samuel Searches for a New King
I Samuel 16: 1-5

The LORD said to Samuel, "How long will you grieve for Saul? I have rejected him? Now I will send you to Jesse, the Bethlehemite. I have provided me a king from one of his sons." Samuel said, "If I go and Saul finds out, he will kill me." The LORD said, "Take a heifer with you and say I am come to sacrifice to the LORD. Then call Jesse to sacrifice and I will show you what to do and you will anoint the one whom I name." Samuel did as the LORD said. The elders of the town trembled and said, "Comest thou peacefully?" He said, "Yes, peacefully." Now he sanctified (made holy) Jesse and his sons and called them to sacrifice.

Samuel Chooses the Youngest Son of Jesse
I Samuel 16: 6-12

Samuel saw Eliab and said, "Surely this is the LORD's anointed before me because of his appearance: good looking, tall." The LORD refused Eliab. He said, "For man looketh on the outward appearance, but the LORD looketh on the heart." Then Jesse called for his other sons: Abinadab and Shammah. Again, Jesse made seven of his sons pass before Samuel.

Samuel said, "The LORD has not chosen these. Do you have any other children?" He said, "I have yet the youngest; he keepeth the sheep." Samuel said, "Fetch him." When Samuel saw him, he was ruddy, had a beautiful countenance, and goodly to look at. And the LORD said, "Arise, anoint him for this is he."

David Anointed
I Samuel 16: 13

He did anoint David and the Spirit of the LORD came upon David from that day forward. So Samuel rose up and went to Ramah.

The LORD's Spirit Leaves Saul
I Samuel 16: 14-18

The Spirit of the LORD left Saul and an evil spirit from the LORD troubled him. His servants said, "Let us seek out a man who plays a harp and let him play for you when the evil spirit is upon thee. You shall feel well." Saul said, "Bring him to me to play the harp. He is Jesse's son, and the LORD is with him."

Saul Calms When David Plays the Harp
I Samuel 16: 19-23

Saul sent for David. Jesse took an ass laden with bread, a bottle of wine, and a kid and sent them by David to Saul. Saul loved David. Saul sent to Jesse saying, "Let David, I pray thee, stand before me, for he hath found favor in my sight." And it came to pass, when the evil spirit was upon Saul, David would play his harp. So Saul was refreshed, and was well, and the evil spirit left him.

The Philistines Went to Battle
1 Samuel 17:1-16

The Philistines came to battle. Saul and the men of Israel gathered together and pitched by the valley of Elah. The Philistines stood on one mountain, Israel stood on a mountain on the other side, a valley between them. Goliath was a giant that stood over 9 feet tall; very big and wore a lot of armor. His spear was huge and he stood and cried out to Israel, "Why are ye come out to set your battle in array? Am not I a Philistine, and ye servants of Saul? Choose a man, and let him come down to me, to fight me, to kill me, and we will be your servants, but if you fail, then you will be our servants." When Saul and all Israel heard this, they were afraid. Jesse had eight sons and the three oldest followed Saul to the battle. David, the youngest, returned from Saul to feed his father's sheep at Bethlehem. The Philistines drew near.

David Takes Food to His Brothers
I Samuel 17: 17-22

Jesse told David to take corn and ten loaves to the camp of his brothers. Saul and all the men of Israel were fighting the Philistines. David rose up early and left; he left the sheep with a keeper. He saw the fighting in the battle, the Philistines, and Israel. David ran into the army and saluted his brothers.

David Sees Goliath
I Samuel 17:23-30

David saw the man Goliath of the Philistines and he heard his words. All the men of Israel when they saw him fled and were sore afraid. They said, "Have you seen this man? Surely, if any man killeth him, the king will make him rich, and will give him his daughter." David said, "What shall be done to the man that killeth him? Who is this uncircumcised Philistine that he should defy the armies of the living God?" And David's oldest brother, Eliab, was angered when he heard David talking to the men. He said, "Why come here? Who did you leave the sheep with? I know the pride and naughtiness of your heart; you just want to see the battle." David said, "What have I done? Is there not a cause?" He turned from him and spoke the same and they did answer him.

David is a Brave Lad
I Samuel 17: 31-39

When it was told to Saul what David spoke, Saul sent for him. David said, "Let no man's heart fail because of him; I will go fight the Philistine." Saul said, "You are but a youth and not able to fight him." David said, "I kept my father's sheep and a lion and a bear took a lamb out of the flock. I went after them and slew them both. And this uncircumcised Philistine shall be as one of them. The LORD that delivered me out of the paw of the lion and the bear, will deliver me out of the hand of the Philistine." Saul said, "Go, and the LORD be with you." Saul armed David with his armor. David said, "I cannot go with these and he took them off."

David and His Sling
I Samuel 17: 40-54

David took his staff in his hand, chose five smooth stones out of the brook and put them in his shepherd's bag, and his sling and went near to the Philistine. When Goliath saw David, he disdained him (with contempt) for he was but a youth. He said to David, "Am I a dog that you come to me with staves?" The Philistine cursed David by his gods. He said, "Come to me; I will give your flesh to the fowls of the air and beasts of the field." David said, "You come to me with a sword, a spear, and with a shield: but I come to you in the name of the LORD of hosts. This day the LORD will deliver you into my hands; I will smite you and the carcass of the Philistines will go to the fowls of the air and wild beasts." When Goliath arose to meet David, he ran and took a stone and slung it and hit him in the forehead and he fell to the ground. David stood on the Philistine, took his sword and slew him, and cut off his head. The Philistines fled. David took the Philistines head to Jerusalem. He put his armor in his tent.

David, Son of Jesse
I Samuel 17: 55-58

Saul wanted to know whose son David is. David returned before Saul and brought the head of the Philistine. David told Saul, "I am the son of Jesse, the Bethlehemite."

The Souls of David and Saul's Son, Jonathan
I Samuel 18: 1-4

When David finished talking with Saul, the soul of Jonathan, Saul's son, was knit with the soul of David. Johnathan loved David. Saul would not let David go home. Jonathan stripped off his robe and put it on David and even gave him his sword, his bow, and girdle.

Saul Is Jealous and Afraid of David
I Samuel 18: 5-16

David went wherever Saul sent him. He went out to war. He was accepted of all the people and Saul's servants. When David returned, the women came out singing and dancing to meet King Saul. The women said, "Saul hath slain his thousands, and David his ten thousands." So Saul was jealous and Saul eyed David from that day forward. It came to pass, the evil spirit came upon Saul and he cast a javelin at David to kill him. David avoided him twice. Saul was afraid of David because the LORD was with him. All of Israel and Judah loved David.

1 Samuel 18:17-30

Saul sent David out hoping the Philistines would kill him. He was to give David his oldest daughter, Merab, for David to wed, but he gave her to a Meholathite. And Michal, Saul's daughter loved David and this pleased Saul. He said, "I will give her to David to snare him, and the hand of the Philistines will be against him." He had his servants to tell David they all love him and Saul wants him to be his son-in-law. For a dowry, because David was a poor man, Saul wants the foreskin of 100 Philistines. But he thought David would die. David arose and slew 200 men and brought their foreskins to Saul. Saul gave him Michal to be his wife. Saul became more afraid of David and became David's enemy continually.

I Samuel 19

Saul was always trying to kill David. But God was always with David. David wrote Psalm 18:19 when the battle ended. "He delivered me because he delighted in me." Jonathan and David's wife Michael loved David and risked their lived to save him.

Michal, David's Wife, Saves Him
I Samuel 19: 11-21

Saul sent messengers to David's house to watch him, to slay him in the morning. Michal, his wife, told him, "If thou save not thy life tonight, tomorrow thou shalt be slain." Michal let David down through a window; he fled and escaped. Michal took an image, and laid it in the bed, put a pillow of goats' hair for his bolster, and covered it with a cloth. Michal told Saul's messengers David is sick. Then Saul told the messengers to bring David to him in his bed, so I may slay him. When they came back, they saw the image in the bed, with the goats' hair. Saul asked Michal, "Why hast thou deceived me so, and sent away mine enemy, that he is escaped?" David fled, and escaped, and came to Samuel and told him all that Saul had done to him. He and Samuel went and dwelt in Naioth. It was told to Saul that David is in Naioth. Saul sent messengers to take David. When they saw the company of the prophets prophesying, and Samuel standing as appointed over them, the Spirit of God was upon them, and they also prophesied. Saul sent messengers two more times and they also prophesied.

I Samuel 20:3

David told Jonathan, "Your father knows I have found grace in your eyes." David and Jonathan wondered if Saul really wanted to kill David.

The Covenant Between Jonathan and David
I Samuel 20: 14-23

Jonathan loved David as he loved his own soul. "Tomorrow at the new moon, you will be missed. When you have been gone three days, I will come to the place where you hide. I will shoot three arrows at the mark. I will send a lad saying, 'Go, find the arrows.' If I say, 'The arrows are on this side of thee, take them,' then come out for there is peace. But if I say, 'Behold, the arrows are beyond thee,' go, for the LORD hath sent thee away."

Saul Misses David
I Samuel 20: 24-34

Saul sat down to eat and asked where David is? He said to Jonathan, "The son of Jesse did not come to eat yesterday or today." Jonathan said, "David earnestly asked to go to Bethlehem. He went home to sacrifice in the city." Saul's anger was kindled against Jonathan. "Do you not know that as long as he liveth upon the ground, you will not be established. Now, send for him, for he shall surely die." Jonathan said, "What has he done? Why shall he be slain?" Saul threw a javelin at him and he knew Saul would slay David. Jonathan was grieved for David.

Jonathan and David Depart from Each Other
I Samuel 20: 35-42

In the morning, Jonathan and the lad went out in the field. And he did as the covenant between himself and David said. Jonathan told the lad to take the artillery to the city. As soon as he was gone, David came out, fell on the ground, and bowed himself three times. They kissed and wept. Jonathan told David to go in peace. "The LORD be between me and thee and my seed and your seed." And Jonathan went back to the city.

***Saul was jealous of David and always tried to kill him. David lived around ten years in exile because he was in constant danger from Saul.

I Samuel 24

David had a chance to kill Saul but said he would not kill God's anointed. David talked with Saul and said, "The LORD judges between us, but my hand shall not be upon you. The LORD will be judge." Saul said, "Is this the voice of my son David?" Saul lifted his voice and wept. "I have rewarded you evil and you rewarded me good. I know you shall be king. Swear to me by the LORD, that you will not cut off the seed after me and you will not destroy my name." David did swear to Saul.

Samuel's Death and Burial
I Samuel 25: 1

Samuel died. All the Israelite's gathered and lamented (mourned) him and buried him in his house at Ramah. And David arose and went down to the wilderness of Paran.

Saul Inquires of a Woman of Spirits
I Samuel 28: 1-11

The Philistines are closing in. God was not with Saul. Saul was not prepared; his prayers are not answered. Samuel was dead and buried. Saul had no one to talk to. He saw the Philistines and he was afraid and trembled. The LORD did not answer him. Saul said to his servants, "Seek me a woman that has familiar spirits, that I may go and enquire of her." Saul disguised himself, put on other clothes; he and two other men went and came to the woman at night. He said, "I pray thee, use your spirit, and bring him up that I name." She said, "You know Saul cut off all those that have familiar spirits, and wizards, so you lay a snare for my life to cause me to die?" Saul swore to her by the LORD, saying, "No punishment will come to you." She said, "Whom shall I bring up?" He said, "Bring me up Samuel."

Samuel Ascended from the Grave
I Samuel 28: 12-14

When the woman saw Samuel, she cried with a loud voice. "Why has thou deceived me? For you are Saul." The king said, "Do not be afraid. What do you see?" She said, "Gods ascending out of the earth." He said, "What form is he of?" She said, "An old man." Saul felt it was Samuel. He stooped his face to the earth and bowed himself.

Saul and Samuel
I Samuel 28: 15-25

Samuel said, "Why have you disturbed me, to bring me up?" Saul said, "I am sore distressed. The Philistines make war against me and the LORD God is departed from me. I called you so that you might tell me what to do." Samuel said, "Then you ask me, seeing the LORD has departed from you and is now your enemy because you did not obey, nor executed Amalek, that's why the LORD has done this. The LORD will deliver you tomorrow into the hands of the Philistines. Tomorrow you and your sons will be with me." Then Saul fell straightway along the earth and was sore afraid. There was no strength in him, he had not eaten all day or night. The woman came to Saul and said to him, "I have put my life in your hands. Let me put bread before you that you may eat and gain your strength." He refused, but the woman and his servants compelled him. They did prepare food and he did eat.

Saul's Death
I Samuel 31: 1-7

The Philistines fought against Israel; the men fled. The Philistines followed hard upon Saul and his sons. They did kill Saul's sons. Saul asked his armourbearer to kill him with his sword and he wouldn't. So Saul took a sword and fell upon it. When the armourbearer saw Saul dead, he fell also upon his sword. They all died that day.

The Philistines Disrespect Saul's Body
I Samuel 31: 8-10

When the Philistines found Saul's body the next day, they cut off his head, stripped off his armor, and sent his body to the land of the Philistines to punish it in the house of their idols. They put his armor in the house of Ashtaroth. They fastened his body to the wall of Bethsham.

Saul's Burial
I Samuel 31: 11-13

When the inhabitants of Jabeshgilead heard what they did to Saul, all the valiant men arose and went by night and took Saul's body and his son's bodies from the wall of Bethshan and burnt them there and they took their bones and buried them under a tree in Jabesh and fasted for seven days.

Lesson 2

A Few Highlights about King David

OK!!!! King Saul has died and his bones buried. So far King Saul is one of my least favorite people in the Bible. David, the young shepherd boy, youngest son of Jesse, becomes king about 7 ½ years after the death of Saul. David was the 2nd and greatest king of Israel. He was a man after God's own heart. His dynasty ruled Judah for over 400 years. He, like Jesus, was also born in Bethlehem. David played the harp for good old Saul to calm his evil ways. He was called a hero after killing Goliath, the Philistine giant. His downfall was watching Bathsheba from the roof and committing adultery with her, and then having her husband murdered after Bathsheba was with child by David. He is remembered as the "Sweet Psalmist of Israel." He wrote many of the psalms.

Concerning Saul's Death
II Samuel 1: 1-12

A man came out of the camp of Saul. He rent his clothes. When he came to David, he fell to the earth and did obeisance (expressed respect). David asked where he came from and he said he had escaped out of the camp of Israel. " I have come to tell you the people fled; many are dead. Saul and Jonathan, his son, are dead also." David said, "How do you know this?" He said, "I happened by chance upon mount Gilboa. Behold, Saul was leaned upon his spear. When he saw me, he called unto me. I said, 'Here am I.' He said, 'Who are you?' I answered, 'I am an Amalekite.' Saul said, 'I pray thee, stand on me and slay me for anguish is on me.' So I stood upon him and slew him because I was sure he could not live after he had fallen. I took his crown and bracelet and have brought them to my lord." Then David did rent his clothes, as well as the men that were with him.

The Young Amalekite Killed
II Samuel 1: 13-16

David said, "Who are you?" He answered, "I am the son of a stranger, an Amalekite." David said, "Were you not afraid to stretch forth your hand to destroy the LORD's anointed?" David called one of his young men and told him to go near and fall upon him. And he died. David said, "Your blood is upon your head for your mouth has testified against you saying, 'I have slain the LORD's anointed.'"

David Made King of Judah
II Samuel 2: 1-11

The LORD told David to go up to the cities of Judah to Hebron. So David, his two wives, and the men that were with him went. And he dwelt in the cities of Hebron. David settled in Hebron after the death of Saul and ruled over Judah for 7½ years. This was before being anointed king over Israel. Saul's son Ishbosheth was 40 years old when he began to rule over Israel and reigned two years. But the house of Judah followed David.

***Hebron was a well-known town when Abraham entered Canaan.

***Saul's cousin Abner was introduced to David after David killed Goliath. Ishbosheth was king after Saul died and Abner was the commander of Saul's army.

II Samuel 3:6-8

Abner's men and David's men fought each other in battle. And after about two years, King Ishbosheth accused Abner of sleeping with Saul's concubine. Abner became angry because it was false. Therefore, Abner promised to turn all of Israel over to David.

David, To Be King of Israel
II Samuel 3: 17-21

Abner told the elders of Israel, "Ye sought for David in times past to be king over you. Now then do it." Abner came to David to Hebron and 20 men with him. David made them a feast. Abner said, "I will arise and go, and will gather all Israel unto my LORD the king. Thou may reign over all that your heart desires." David sent him away in peace.

***Joab was a Jewish military commander under King David.

Joab Slew Abner
II Samuel 3: 22-30

Joab and the servants of David came from pursuing a troop. Abner was not with David in Hebron. David had sent him away in peace. Joab said, "What hast thou done? Why did you send him away? You know Abner came to deceive you, just to know your coming and goings." When Joab was out from David, he sent messengers after Abner; they brought him back, but David did not know. Then Joab took Abner aside to speak to him. He smote him under the 5th rib, and he died. When David heard, he said, "I and my kingdom are guiltless before the LORD forever from the blood of Abner. Joab and his brother slew Abner because he had killed their brother." David did mourn for Abner.

***The Covenant is like a contract between God and His people. It was a guide to who the Israelites were to worship, how to engage with non-Israelites, or how to deal with things of their life.

***Covenant: The conditional promises made to humanity by God, as revealed in Scripture. The agreement between God and the ancient Israelites in which God promised to protect them if they were faithful to Him and kept His law.

Ishbosheth's Death
II Samuel 4: 1-8

Rachab and Baanah went to the house of Ishbosheth, who lay on his bed at noon. They came in and smote him, and beheaded him, and took his head to David. They said it was because his father Saul was your enemy and wanted to kill you.

The Death of the Two That Killed Ishbosheth
II Samuel 4: 9-12

David said, "As the LORD liveth, who hath redeemed my soul out of all diversity? When one came telling me Saul was dead, thinking they brought me good tidings, I took hold of him and slew him. Who would have thought I would give him a reward. How much more is it, when wicked men have slain a righteous man in his own house upon his bed? I will now require your blood and take you away from this earth." David commanded his young men, and they slew them, cut off their hands and feet, and hanged them up over the pool in Hebron. They took the head of Ishbosheth and buried it.

David Anointed as King of Israel
II Samuel 5: 1-5

The tribes of Israel to David, "Behold, we are thy bone and thy flesh. In time past when Saul was king, you led us out and brought us to Israel." So all the elders of Israel came to Hebron before the LORD. And they anointed David king over Israel. David was 30 years old and he reigned 40 years.

Jerusalem Made Capital of Israel
II Samuel 5: 6-12

King David and his men went to Jerusalem unto the Jebusites. They told him he can't come in. But David took the stronghold of Zion, the same is the city of David. David conquered Jerusalem by a surprise assault and Jerusalem was made the capital of Israel, the city of David.

A Temple for the Ark
II Samuel 7: 1-3

King David sat in his house, and the LORD had given him rest from all his enemies. David said to <u>Nathan the prophet</u>, "See now, I dwell in a house of cedar, but the ark of God dwelleth within curtains." Nathan said, "Go, do all you want, the LORD is with thee." David had a desire to build a house for the ark of God. The LORD had a more loving thought in mind: a more glorious house, an everlasting dynasty.

David's Greatness and Kindness
II Samuel 9: 1-8

David reigned over all Israel, he executed judgment and justice to all his people. David asked, "Is there yet anyone left in the house of Saul that I may show him kindness for Jonathan's sake."

***Remember Jonathan and David's soul were as the same, they loved each other.

They said, "Jonathan has a son which is lame on his feet." He said, "Where is he?" David sent for him. His name is Mephibosheth. They brought him to David. He was expecting to be killed. He fell on his face and said, "Behold thy servant!" David said, "Fear not, I will surely show you kindness for Jonathan's sake. And I will restore all the land of Saul thy father. And you shall eat bread at my table continually."

David Sees Beautiful Bathsheba
II Samuel 11: 1-13

David sent Joab and his servants and all Israel to battle. In the evening, David went upon the roof. He saw a very beautiful woman washing herself. David sent and inquired about her. One said, "Is not this Bathsheba, the daughter of Eliam, the wife of Uriah the Hittite?" David sent messengers and took her; she came in unto David, and he lay with her. She was purified (to free from guilt or evil) and she returned to her house. She conceived. She sent word to David and said, "I am with child." David said to Joab, "Send me Uriah (husband of Bathsheba.)" When Uriah came to him, David said, "Go down to your house, and wash thy feet." But Uriah slept at the door of the king's house and did not go to his house. He said to David, "The ark, Israel, and Judah abide in tents, and my lord Joab, and the servant of my lord are encamped in the open fields. Shall I then go to my house, to eat and drink and lie with my wife? As thou livest and as my soul liveth, I will not do this thing." David said, "Tarry here today, and tomorrow I will let you depart." So Uriah did so. When David called him, he did eat and drink before him and he made him drunk. At evening he went to lie on his bed with the servants of his lord but did not go to his house to see his wife.

Uriah's Death
II Samuel 11: 14-17

Come morning, David wrote a letter to Joab and sent it by Uriah. He wrote, "Set ye Uriah in the front line of the hottest battle, and retire ye from him, that he may die." Joab did as David said. The men of the city went out and fought with Joab. Uriah the Hittite died. They told king David that Uriah is dead. When Bathsheba heard her husband was dead, she mourned. When the mourning passed, David sent for her and she became his wife.

***But the thing David had done displeased the LORD.

A Parable from the LORD
II Samuel 12: 1-6

The LORD sent Nathan to David. He said, "There were two men in one city: one man was rich and one was poor. The rich man had exceeding many flocks and herds. The poor man had nothing but one little ewe lamb (female sheep) which he had bought and nourished up. It grew with him and his children, it ate of his own meat, drank from his own cup, and lay in his bosom and was like a daughter. A traveler came to the rich man who spared (refrained from) to take of his own flock or his own herd to dress for the wayfaring man. But he took the poor man's lamb and dressed it for the man. David's anger was greatly kindled against the man and he said to Nathan, "As the LORD liveth, the man that hath done this thing shall surely die. And he shall restore the lamb fourfold because he did this thing, and because he had no pity."

David's Sin Exposed by Nathan
II Samuel 12: 7-12

Nathan said to David, "You are that man." This saith the LORD God of Israel, "I anointed you king over Israel, delivered you out of the hand of Saul, wives, and much more. You have despised the commandments of the LORD, to do evil in his sight? You killed Uriah the Hittite with the sword and have taken his wife, and hast slain him with the sword of the children of Ammon. Now therefore the sword shall never depart from thine house because thou hast despised me and hast taken the wife of Uriah, to be thy wife. I will raise up evil against you out of your own house. I will take your wives and give them to your neighbor, and he shall lie with your wives in your sight. You did it secretly, but I will do this thing before all Israel, and before the sun."

David Repents
II Samuel 12: 13-17

David said to Nathan, "I have sinned against the LORD." Nathan said, "The LORD has put away your sin; you shall not die. But, because of this deed, to blaspheme, the child also that is born to you shall die." Nathan departed to his house. The LORD struck the child of Bathsheba, and it was very sick. David besought God for the child, he fasted, and lay all night upon the earth. The elders went to help him up, he did not get up or eat.

David's Child Dies
II Samuel 12: 18-19

And on the seventh day, the child died. The servants feared to tell him. But when he perceived the child was dead, David asked, "Is the child dead?" They said, "He is dead."

David Worships the LORD After His Son Died
II Samuel 12: 20-23

David arose from the earth and washed and anointed himself,

changed his clothes, and worshiped. Then he came to his own house and he ate. The servants said, "What thing is it you have done? You did fast and weep for the child while it was alive, but when the child died, you rose and eat bread." David said, "While he was alive, I fasted and wept saying, 'Who can tell if God will be gracious to me, that the child may live.' But now he is dead. Why should I fast? Can I bring him back??"

Solomon's Birth
II Samuel 12: 24

David comforted Bathsheba, his wife. He went in unto her and lay with her. She bare him a son and called him Solomon and the LORD loved him.

II Samuel 13

This is a chapter of love that turns to hate, revenge, and grief. It is about three of David's children. Amnon loved his half-sister Tamar and tricked her into coming into his bedroom and he raped her. Then he hated her. Absalom, their brother, ended up killing Amnon for raping his sister.

Psalm 51

READ: This is a Psalm David wrote when Nathan the prophet came unto him after David had gone in unto Bathsheba.

Lesson 3

David Wants a Census
II Samuel 24: 1-9

And again, the anger of the LORD was kindled against Israel. David was full of pride and Satan seized upon that. David wanted a census so he could boast about the number of people. God was in control, and he did allow it to happen, so to bring David to a place of humility, so he would know the reality of what he was doing. Taking a census was not wrong, but David was prideful. God wanted David to grow in the LORD. Satan always wants to discredit and deceive.

*** The eternal sin (blasphemy against the Holy Spirit) is one sin God hates and it is considered as the sin unto death. Also, pride, as mentioned above, is a sin God hates.

Proverbs 16:5 Every one that is proud in heart is an abomination to the LORD; though hand join in hand, he shall not be unpunished.

David Repents
II Samuel 24: 10-17

David's heart smote him (brought him down) after he had numbered the people. He told the LORD, "I have sinned greatly in what I have done. O LORD, take away the iniquity of thy servant for I have done very foolishly." When David got up in the morning, the word of the LORD came unto the prophet Gad, saying, "Go and say to David, 'Thus saith the LORD, I offer thee three things. Choose one that I may do it unto thee.' Shall seven years of famine come unto thee in thy land? Or wilt thou flee three months before your enemies while they pursue thee? Or that there be three days of pestilence in thy land? Now advise and see what answer I shall tell the LORD." David said to Gad, "I am in a great strait (difficulty, distraught). Let us fall now into the hand of the LORD for his mercies are great. And let me not fall into the hand of man." The LORD sent a pestilence upon Israel from the morning even to the time appointed and from Dan to Beersheba, 70,000 men died.

Don't Destroy Jerusalem
II Samuel 24: 16-17

The LORD told the angel not to destroy Jerusalem. He said, "The people that were destroyed is enough." David spake unto the LORD when he saw the angel that smote the people and said, "Lo, I have sinned and I have done wickedly but these sheep, what have they done? I pray thee, let your hand be against me and my brother's house."

Araunah's Threshing Floor is Bought
II Samuel 24: 18-25

Gad came to David and said, "Go up, rear (to raise by building) an altar unto the LORD in the threshing floor of Arunah the Jebusite. David went and Araunah saw him coming. Araunah bowed himself on the ground. Araunah said, "Why has my lord the king come?" David said, "To buy your threshing floor, to build and altar unto the LORD, that the plague may stay away from the people. Make me an offer that seemeth good. Behold, here is oxen for burnt sacrifice, and threshing instruments, and other instruments of the oxen for wood."

Araunah said he would give all this to David, and he said to the king, "The LORD thy God accept thee." And the king said, "Nay, but I will surely buy it from you at a price. I won't offer burnt offerings to the LORD my God of that which doesn't cost me anything." David bought the threshing floor and oxen for 50 shekels of silver ($25,000). David built an altar unto the LORD. He offered burnt offerings and peace offerings. So the LORD was intreated for the land, and the plague was stayed from Israel.

Declining Health
I Kings 1: 1-4

King David was old and stricken in years. They covered him, but he didn't get warm. His servants said, "Let us get a young virgin. Let her stand before the king, let her cherish you, and let her lie in your bosom that my lord may get some heat." So Abishag, a Shunamite, was brought to the king. She was very fair and cherished the king and ministered to him, but the king knew her not.

Adonijah Claims Himself as King
I Kings 1: 5-14

Adonijah, the son of Haggith, exalted himself saying he is going to be king. Nathan spoke to Bathsheba, the mother of Solomon, and said, "Hast thou not heard that Adonijah doth reign and David knoweth it not? Go tell King David, and ask if he did not, my lord, O king, swear to me that assuredly Solomon thy son will reign after you, and sit upon thy throne? Why then does Adonijah reign?" Nathan said, "While you talk to the king, I will also come and confirm thy words."

***Haggith was one of King David's wives.

***<u>II Samuel 3:4</u> And the fourth, Adonijah, the son of Haggith.

David Assures Bathsheba
I Kings 1: 28-31

King David said, "Call Bathsheba." She stood before the king. The king sware, "As the LORD liveth, even as I swear unto you by the LORD God of Israel, assuredly Solomon thy son shall reign after me, and sit upon my throne in my stead, even so today." Bathsheba bowed her head and did reverence to the king.

About Solomon

Solomon was the second child of David and Bathsheba. He asked God for an understanding mind, to be able to recognize the difference between good and evil. God was pleased with what he asked for. He was a very intelligent man. He departed from his religion and was chastised by God. He built the temple in seven years. He built shrines for his heathen wives to worship their false gods.

Solomon Gets Advice from David
I Kings 2: 1-9

The days of David drew nigh that he shall die. He said to Solomon, "Be strong, and be a man. Keep the charge of the LORD thy God, walk in his ways, keep his statutes, his commandments, his judgments, his testimonies, as it is written in the law of Moses, that wherever you go or what you do, you will prosper."

David's Reign, Death, and Burial
I Kings 2: 10-11

So David slept with his fathers and was buried in the city of David. He reigned over Israel 40 years, Hebron for seven years, and Jerusalem for 33 years.

Solomon's Wisdom
I Kings 3: 6-15

Solomon said, "You have shown thy servant David my father great mercy. He walked before you in truth, in righteousness, in uprightness of heart with thee and thou has given him a son to sit on his throne. Now, O LORD my God, I am thy servant king, instead of David my father. I am but a little child. I know not how to go out or come in. I am in the midst of a great people, that cannot be numbered. Give me an understanding heart to judge thy people that I may discern between good and bad for who is able to judge this thy so great people?"

God is Pleased with Solomon's Request
I Kings 3:10-15

The speech pleased the LORD. The LORD said, "Because you didn't ask for long life, riches, nor ask the life of thine enemies, but asked for understanding, behold, I have done according to thy words. I have also given thee which you didn't ask for: riches and honor. There shall not be any among the kings like you, and if you walk in my ways to keep my statues and my commandments as thy father did, then I will lengthen thy days." Then Solomon awoke and it was a dream. He came to Jerusalem and stood before the ark of the covenant of the LORD and offered up burnt offerings and offered peace offerings and made a feast for all his servants.

A Living Child and a Dead Child
I Kings 3: 16-22

Two harlots came to the king. One woman said, "O my lord, I and this woman dwell in one house. I delivered a child with her in the house. And three days after, this woman delivered also. There was no one in the house with us. This woman's child died in the night because she laid on it. Then she arose at midnight and took my son while I slept and laid it in her bosom, and she laid her dead child with me. When I woke in the morning to give my baby suck, behold, it was dead. It was not my son." And the other woman said, "Nay, but the living is my son, and the dead is her son; the living is mine."

Solomon Makes a Wise Decision
I Kings 3: 23-28

The king said, "Bring me a sword. "Divide the living child in two and give half to one, and half to the other." The one woman who had the living child said, "O my lord, give her the living child, and in no wise slay it." The other woman said, "Divide the child." Then the king answered and said, "Give her the living child, for she is the mother." All Israel heard of the judgment; they feared the king for they saw the wisdom of God was in him to do judgment.

The Temple is Constructed
I Kings 6:1

And it came to pass, 480 years after the children of Israel came out of Egypt, King Solomon began to build the house of the LORD.

Solomon's Downfall
I Kings 11: 1-3

King Solomon loved many strange women: the daughter of Pharaoh, women of the Moabites, Ammonites, Edomites, Zidonians, and Hittites. God had told the children of Israel, "Ye shall not go into them. Neither shall they come into you. They will turn away your heart after their gods." Solomon loved these women.

Solomon Builds Idols for His Wives
I Kings 11: 4-8

When Solomon was old, his wives turned his heart to other gods. His heart was not perfect with the LORD his God. He did evil in the sight of the LORD, as David his father.

God's Anger Toward Solomon
I Kings 11: 9-13

The LORD was angry with Solomon because his heart was turned from the LORD God of Israel. The LORD told him, "You should not go after other gods. Because you have done this, I will surely rend the kingdom from you and give it to thy servant."

Solomon's Death and Burial
I Kings 11: 41-43

Solomon slept with his fathers, he was buried in the City of David, his father. And Rehoboam, his son, reigned in his stead.

Rehoboam
I Kings 12: 1-5

Rehoboam went to Shechem. All Israel came to make him king. He had fled from King Solomon. He and all the congregation of Israel came. They spoke to him, "Your father made our yoke grievous. Will you please make our yoke lighter, and we will serve you?"
He said, "Depart from me for three days, then come back and I will give you my answer."

Rehoboam Consults with the Men
Genesis 12:6-11

Rehoboam consulted with the old men. They said, "If you will be a servant to the people, and will serve them, speak good words to them, then they will be your servants forever." Then he consulted with the younger men he grew up with. They said, "Tell the people that said your father made their yoke heavy, I will add to your yoke. My father chastised you with whips, but I will chastise you with scorpions." So he didn't listen to the old men but listened to the young men. FAST FORWARD>>>>>>> When he refused to lighten Solomon's policy of heavy taxation and forced labor, the northern tribes seceded (withdrew) from his kingdom. Only the southern tribes of Judah and Benjamin stayed under Rehoboam in what became the Kingdom of Judah. (II Chronicles 12:16) And Rehoboam slept with his father in the City of David. He was 41 years old when he began to reign and he reigned 17 years.

Abijam, Rehoboam's Son
I Kings 15: 1-8

Abijam reigned three years in Jerusalem. He walked in all the sins of his father. His heart was not perfect with the LORD his God, as the heart of David. But, for David's sake the LORD his God gave him a lamp in Jerusalem to set up his son after him, to establish Jerusalem. Abijam slept with his fathers and was buried in the City of David. Asa his son reigned in his stead.

Asa Loves the LORD and Follows Him
I Kings 15: 9

Asa reigned over Judah 41 years. Asa did that which was right in the eyes of the LORD, as David his father. He removed all the idols his father had made. He removed his mother from being queen because she had made an idol. He destroyed her idol and burnt it. His heart was perfect with the LORD all his days. At the time of his old age, he was diseased in his feet. And Asa slept with his fathers and was buried with his fathers in the City of David. And then, Jehoshaphat his son reigned.

Nadab's Reign and Fall
1 Kings 15: 25-32

Nadab, son of Jeroboam, began to reign over Israel in the second year of Asa, king of Judah. He reigned two years. He did evil in the sight of the LORD. And Baasha, the son of Ahijah, conspired against him. And Baasha smote him at Gibbethon. It came to pass, when he reigned, he smote all the house of Jeroboam. He left none of them.

The Temple Destroyed
II Chronicles 36:18-19

The King of Babylonia, Nebuchadnezzar II, sent in forces and served a deadly blow to the rebellious kingdom of Judah. They destroyed the holy temple, The Temple of Solomon, in 586 BC. And he burnt the house of the LORD, and the king's house, and all the houses of Jerusalem, and every great man's house burnt he with fire.

II Chronicles 36: 21

To fulfill the word of the LORD by mouth of Jeremiah, until the land had enjoyed her Sabbaths: for as long as she lay desolate, she kept the sabbath for 70 years.

***The temple was robbed and destroyed. The people hoped for God's protection. It was too late. The temple was now a den of thieves, not a house of prayer.

Lesson 4

The people of Israel wanted a king. God warned them of challenges. There was a great divide in about the 10th century BCE (before common era). The kingdoms of Israel and Judah split. The tribes of Judah and Benjamin did not agree or have the same opinion as King Rehoboam. They forsake their inheritance and became the Southern Kingdom of Judah. The northern 10 tribes stayed the tribe of Israel. They fought each other. They were strong but they both fell into captivity. The Babylonians captured Judah and they stayed in captivity 70 years. The Assyrians captured Israel and they never fully came out of captivity.

Cyrus' Proclamation
II Chronicles 36: 22-23 & Ezra 1: 1-4

In the first year of Cyrus, king of Persia, the word spoken of Jeremiah might be accomplished, the LORD stirred up the spirit of Cyrus, that he made a proclamation throughout all his kingdom. Thus saith Cyrus, "All kingdoms of the earth hath the LORD God of heaven given me and he hath charged me to build him a house in Jerusalem, which is in Judah. Who is there among you of all his people? The LORD his God be with him and let him go up."

Coming Out of Captivity
Ezra 2: 1

These are the children of the province that went up out of captivity that had been carried away by Nebuchadnezzar, king of Babylon. They came with Zerubbabel.

***Ezra 2: 2-63 Names the people that came up out of captivity.

Foundation Completed for the Temple
Ezra 3: 8-11

In the second year, Zerubbabel and Jeshua, the remnant of their brethren, the priest and the Levites, and all that came out of captivity unto Jerusalem and appointed the Levites, from 20 years and older to set forth the work of the house of the LORD. They began the work and laid the foundation of the temple of the LORD. They shouted with a great shout when they praised the LORD because the foundation was laid.

***Jonah was a Hebrew prophet, son of Amittai. God told Jonah to go to Nineveh to preach to the people about their sinful ways. Jonah didn't want to go and he tried to escape from God.

Jonah 1

God commanded Jonah to go to Nineveh, an ancient capital city of the Assyrian Empire. Jonah rose up and fled to Tarshish. He wanted to get away from God. When he got to Joppa, he found a ship going to Tarshish. The LORD sent a mighty wind into the sea: a mighty tempest, like the ship would break in two. Everyone was afraid and cried out to his god. Jonah had gone down into the sides of the ship and was asleep. The ship master came to him, "What do you mean, O sleeper? Arise, call upon thy God." They cast lots to see whose god caused this evil. The lot fell upon Jonah. He told them that he fled from the LORD. They said, "What shall we do to you, that the sea may be calm." Jonah said, "Cast me forth into the sea." Nevertheless, the men rowed hard to bring it to land, but could not. So, they cast Jonah into the sea, and the sea ceased raging. The men feared God and offered a sacrifice unto the LORD. A great fish did swallow Jonah. He was in the belly of the great fish three days and three nights.

Jonah 2

Jonah prayed and said, "I cried, and you heard me; out of the belly of hell I cried." The LORD spoke unto the fish and it vomited Jonah upon dry land.

Jonah 3

The word of the LORD came to Jonah the second time. "Arise, go to Nineveh." Jonah arose and went. It was a three-day journey. Jonah began to enter into the city, and he cried, "Yet 40 days, and Nineveh shall be overthrown." So the people of Nineveh believed God, they proclaimed a fast, they put on sackcloth, from the greatest to the least.

***Sackcloth- a garment which was worn as a token of mourning by the Israelites. It is often associated with ashes.

Word came to the king of Nineveh. He arose, took off his robe, and covered himself with sackcloth and sat in ashes. He put out a decree saying, "Let man nor beast, herd nor flock, taste anything; let them not eat or drink water. But let them be covered with sackcloth, and cry mightily unto God. Yea, let them turn from his evil way. Who can tell if God will turn and repent, and turn from his fierce anger, that we perish not." God saw their works and that they turned from their evil ways. So God did not do unto them that He had said.

Jonah 4

But it displeased Jonah exceedingly. He was angry. Jonah prayed to the LORD, "Was not this my saying when I was in my country? I know that you are a gracious God, and merciful, slow to anger, and of great kindness, and repentest thee of the evil. Therefore now, O LORD, take, my life from me; for it is better for me to die than to live." The LORD said, "Doest (does it) make you happy to be angry?" Jonah went out of the city on the east side and made a booth and sat under it in the shadow till he might see what would become of the city. The LORD God prepared a gourd, and made a shadow over his head, to deliver him from his grief. Jonah was glad for the gourd. But God prepared a worm and the next day it smote the gourd and it withered. When the sun did rise, God prepared an east wind. The sun beat upon Jonah's head; he fainted and wished himself to die. God said to Jonah, "Doest thou well to be angry for the gourd?" And he said, "I do well to be angry, even unto death." The LORD said, "You had pity on the gourd for which you didn't labor, which came up at night and perished in a night. And should I not spare Nineveh, that great city?"

The Prophets

Isaiah 53

Isaiah predicted the birth of Jesus hundreds of years before he was born.
No beauty, he was despised and rejected, man of sorrows, acquainted with grief. He carried our grief, he was wounded for our transgressions, bruised for our iniquities. He was the Lamb. Isaiah told of Jesus hundreds of years before his birth.

Jeremiah

God called to Jeremiah, "Before I formed thee in the belly, I knew you. I ordained thee a prophet before you came out of the womb." Jeremiah told God's people the Babylonians would conquer them. He mourned after the downfall of Jerusalem and the destruction of the temple. He is known as the Weeping Prophet.

Hosea

God told the prophet Hosea to marry a prostitute named Gomer. She wasn't happy to just be married to Hosea. She would run off with other men and because Hosea loved her, he would go get her and bring her back. This is an illustration of God's love for His people.

***There were many prophets that preached before the destruction of Judah.

Amos

Amos was a shepherd near Bethlehem. He was one of the 12 minor prophets. He predicted the destruction of the northern kingdom of Israel. Amos told them if they didn't repent, they will be destroyed.

Amos 7: 17

Therefore, thus saith the LORD, "Thy wife shall be a harlot in the city, and thy sons and thy daughters shall fall by the sword, and thy land shall be divided by line, and thou shalt die in a polluted land. And Israel shall surely go into captivity forth of his land.

Micah 5: 2

But thou, Bethlehem Ephrathah, though thou be little among the thousands of Judah, yet out of thee shall come forth unto me that is to be ruler in Israel; whose goings forth have been from of old, from everlasting. Micah predicted the birthplace of Jesus.

Habakkuk 2: 4

Behold, his soul which is lifted up is not upright in him but the just shall live by his faith.

Zephaniah

He warned about the Day of the LORD.

Lesson 5

Edom is Judged
Obadiah 1: 1-8

The Edomites are descendants of Esau and enemies of the Israelites. Esau married outside of Israel. He gave up his birthright for a bowl of pottage. The Edomites rejoiced when Jerusalem was destroyed by the Babylonians. God promised to bring them down because of their pride.

***The bad blood between Judah and Edom was from Jacob and Esau.

***Obadiah preached to Edom and told them God would punish and destroy them.

The Prophet's Warnings Ignored by Judah
Jeremiah 25: 1-7

Jeremiah the prophet told Judah and the inhabitants of Jerusalem, "The word of the LORD hath come unto me, and I have spoken unto you, but ye have not hearkened. The prophets have said, 'Turn from your evil way, from evil doings, and dwell in the land that the LORD hath given unto you and your fathers forever and ever. Don't serve other gods, and provoke me to anger, and I will do you no hurt.' Yet, ye have not hearkened unto me, saith the LORD."

The People Will Serve the Babylonians Seventy Years
Jeremiah 25: 8-16

Therefore, saith the LORD, "Because you have not heard my words, I will take all the families of the north, and Nebuchadnezzar, the king of Babylon, will bring them against this land, and will utterly destroy them. The whole land shall be a desolation, and an astonishment, and these nations shall serve the king of Babylon 70 years.

God Will Punish the Babylonians
Jeremiah 25: 12

And it shall come to pass, when 70 years are accomplished that I will punish the king of Babylon and that nation

The Action Sermons
Ezekiel 5: 1-4

Ezekiel was a priest and the word of the LORD came to him. He looked and a whirlwind came out of the north, a great cloud, a fire enfolding itself, and a brightness about it, and out of the midst as the color of amber, out of the midst of the fire. There was a likeness of four living creatures. Read Ezekiel 1:5-28 for a description of the creatures. Ezekiel saw the appearance of the bow in the cloud, the appearance of the likeness of the glory of the LORD. When he saw it, he fell upon his face and the LORD spoke to him. The LORD said, "Son of man, stand and I will speak to you." The Spirit of the LORD entered him. "Son of Man, I send you to the children of Israel, a rebellious nation. They have rebelled against me. They show no respect and they are stiff hearted. Go to them and say, 'Thus said the Lord GOD, if they hear or not, they shall know a prophet has been among them. Be not afraid of them.' God was angry because they had rebelled against Him and defiled His temple.

Daniel is Made Great
Daniel 2: 48-49

Daniel was a great prophet during captivity. The king made Daniel a great man, gave him many great gifts, and made him ruler over the whole province of Babylon. Daniel requested the king set Shadrach, Meshach, and Abednego over the affairs of the province of Babylon. Daniel sat in the gate of the king.

People To Serve the Golden Image
Daniel 3: 1-13

King Nebuchadnezzar made a golden image. He gathered all the people and said, "When you hear the sound of the cornet, flute, harp, all kinds of music, ye shall fall down and worship the golden image or be cast into the midst of a burning fiery furnace." It was told to the king that there are certain Jews whom you have cast over the affairs of the province of Babylon: Shadrach, Meshach, and Abednego. These men, O king, have not regarded thee. They serve not thy gods, nor worship the golden image. Then Nebuchadnezzar, in his rage and fury, commanded they be brought before the king.

The Fiery Furnace Heated Seven Times Hotter
Daniel 3: 14-25

The king spoke to Shadrach, Meshach, and Abednego and asked if it's true that they refuse to serve my gods and worship the golden image? Now, if when you hear the sound of all the music, ye fall down and worship the golden image I have made but if ye do not, ye shall be cast the same hour into the fiery furnace, and who is that God that shall deliver you out of my hands?" They said, "If it be so, God whom we serve is able to deliver us from the fiery furnace, and he will deliver us out of your hand, O king. But if not, let it be known, we will not serve your gods, nor the golden image." Then Nebuchadnezzar was full of fury, and he changed against them. The king commanded to heat the furnace 7 times more. He had the most mighty men in his army to bind Shadrach, Meshach, and Abednego to cast them into the furnace. The men that threw them into the furnace, were slain by the flames. The king was astonished (dazed: bewildered) and rose up in haste and spoke. "Did not we cast 3 men into the midst of the fire. They are not hurt, and the form of the 4th is like the Son of God."

Shadrach, Meshach, and Abednego
Daniel 3: 26-30

The king called for them to come forth. All gathered and saw these men from the fire had no pain, nor was a hair of their head singed, neither their coats changed, nor the smell of fire on them. Then Nebuchadnezzar said, "Blessed be the God of Shadrach, Meshach, and Abednego who hath sent His angel to deliver His servants that trusted Him." He made a decree that if anyone speak against the God of these 3 men, they shall be cut in pieces. Then the king promoted them in the province of Babylon.

King Darius

Darius was king of Babylon. There isn't much known about him. The king of Chaldeans, Belshazzar, was slain and Darius the Mead took the kingdom when he was 62 years old.

Daniel 6: 1-3

Darius sat over the kingdom 120 princes, which should be over the whole kingdom. He made Daniel the first president.

Finding Fault with Daniel
Daniel 6: 4-5

The presidents and princes sought to find occasion against Daniel but couldn't find any fault with him. Then they said, "We will find fault with him concerning the law of his God."

The Royal Decree Signed By King Darius
Daniel 6: 6-9

The president and princes said to the king, "We have consulted together to establish a royal statute and make a firm decree that whosoever shall ask a petition of any God or man for 30 days, but you, O King, shall be cast into the lion's den." King Darius signed the decree.

Daniel Prays Three Times a Day
Daniel 6: 10-15

Daniel knew the decree was signed. He went into the house. His windows were open. He kneeled down three times a day and prayed, and gave thanks before his God, as he did before. The men came before the king. You signed a decree for no one to worship any other God. Daniel, which is of the children of the captivity of Judah, regardeth not thee, O King, but prays three times a day. Then the king was displeased with himself and set his heart to deliver Daniel. And he worried till the going down of the sun to deliver him. These men said the decree may not be changed.

Daniel In the Lion's Den
Daniel 6: 16-21

Then the king commanded, and they brought Daniel and cast him into the den of lions. The king spoke to Daniel, "Thy God whom you serve continually, will deliver thee." The king had a stone brought and he laid it upon the mouth of the den and the king sealed it with his own signet so it could not be changed. Then the king went to his palace, fasted all night, and slept not. Then he arose early and went to the lion's den. He saw Daniel and said, "O Daniel, servant of the living God, is thy God able to deliver you from the lions?" Then said Daniel unto the king, "O King, live forever."

Joel, A Prophet

Joel was the second of the 12 minor prophets of Israel. The word of the LORD came to him. Joel 1:4-12 describes the locust devastation. Joel teaches about praying and fasting.

The LORD's Givings
Joel 2: 25

"And I will restore to you the years that the locust hath eaten, the canker worm, and the caterpillar, and the palmerworm, my great army which I sent among you."

Haggai and Zechariah

Haggai encouraged the workers to finish the temple. His goal was to restore the nation after the Jews left captivity of the Babylonians and came back to their homeland.

Zechariah ministered with Haggai. They both encouraged the Jews to work and rebuild the temple.

Ezra and Nehemiah

These two men were not prophets. Ezra, the scribe, helped in the temple ministry. Nehemiah was a layman. They both trusted God and felt God would guide them.

Malachi

Malachi kept telling the people to depend on God and that one day, they will be rescued. He is the last prophet in the Old Testament.

Four Hundred Years

This was the time between the Old and New Testaments. God was silent during this time. It was a time between Malachi and the advent of Christ.

***Advent of Christ- The period of preparation for the celebration of the birth of Jesus Christ and the preparation for the Second Coming of Christ.

***Cyrus was king of Persia. He is the one that gave the Jews permission to go back to Jerusalem and told them to rebuild their temple

Esther
Esther 2:15

Esther was the daughter of Abihail who was the uncle of Mordecai. She was raised by her uncle Mordecai after her parents died. She became a mighty queen even though she was just an unknown Jewish girl.

The King Demands Queen Vashti's Presence
Esther 1: 1-12

King Ahasuerus had planned a royal feast unto all his princes and his servants. And the drinking was according to the law. The king appointed all the officers of his house, that they should do according to every man's pleasure. Also, Vashti, the queen, made a feast for the women in the royal house which belonged to King Ahasuerus. On the 7th day when the king's heart was merry with wine, he commanded some men that served to bring Vashti the queen, before the king to show the people and princes her beauty. But she refused, and the king was very angry.

The King Punishes His Wife
Esther 1: 13-22

The men asked, "What shall we do to the queen according to law? For this deed, she shall come abroad unto all women, so that they shall despise their husbands in their eyes. He commanded the queen be brought to him; she came not. Let it be written among the laws that Vashti come no more before the king, and the king give her royal estate to someone better. And all the wives shall give in to their husband's honor."

Seeking A New Queen
Esther 2: 1-4

The king said, "Let there be fair virgins sought for the king. Let the maiden which pleaseth the king, be queen." There was a certain Jew named Mordecai. He raised Esther, his uncle's daughter, when her parents had died. She was fair and beautiful. She was brought into the king's house, put in custody of Hegai , keeper of the women. Esther pleased him and obtained kindness of him. He preferred her. Mordecai walked by every day to see what happened to Esther.

Esther Is Chosen
Esther 2: 12-20

After she had been there 12 months, these were the days of her purification. Six months with oil of myrrh, and 6 months with sweet odors. Esther obtained favor in the sight of all that looked upon her. The king loved her above all the women. He set the royal crown upon her head and made her queen. Esther had not yet shown her kindred (Jew). She obeyed Mordecai.

The King Saved by Mordecai
Esther 2: 21-23

Two of the king's chamberlains that kept the door were wroth and sought to kill King Ahasuerus. Mordecai knew this and told Esther the queen. Esther told the king and the two were hanged on a tree.

Haman Hates Mordecai
Esther 3: 1-5

After this, the king promoted Haman to set above all. All the servants at the gate bowed to Haman. But Mordecai bowed not. The king's servants asked him why he bowed not. He told them he was a Jew. When Haman saw that he bowed not, he was full of wrath.

Jews To Be Killed
Esther 3: 6-15

Haman then sought to kill all Jews. He told the king that there is a certain people scattered abroad and dispersed among the provinces of thy kingdom, their laws are not the king's laws. Therefore, it is not for the king's profit to suffer them. If it please the king, let it be written that they may be destroyed. The king took off his ring and gave it to Haman. He said, "The silver is given to thee, the people also. Do to them as you wish." And a letter was sent to all the king's provinces to destroy and kill all Jews.

The Jews Mourn
Esther 4: 1-3

When Mordecai saw all that was done, he rent his clothes, put on sackcloth with ashes, and went out into the city and cried with a loud bitter cry. He came before the king's gate for none might enter into the king's gate clothed with sackcloth. There was great mourning among the Jews: fasting, weeping, wailing, many lay in sackcloth and ashes.

Esther and Mordecai Talk
Esther 4: 4-17

The chamberlains came and told Esther. She sent clothes for Mordecai, but he refused to take off his sackcloth. Esther sent for Hatach, one of the king's chamberlains. He came and she told him to go to Mordecai and find out what is wrong. Mordecai told him, and of the sum of money that Haman had promised to pay the king's treasuries for the Jews to be destroyed. He also gave a copy of the decree to show to Esther that she should tell the king, and to make a request before him for her people. Esther told Hatach to tell Mordecai, "All the king's servants and the people know, and whosoever shall come unto the king unto the inner court who is not called, he shall be put to death." Mordecai told Esther, "Just because you are in the king's house, don't think you will escape." She bade them to tell Mordecai, "Gather together all the Jews that are present, and fast for 3 days. I and my maidens will also, and if I perish, I perish." Mordecai went his way and did as Esther commanded.

Esther's Courage
Esther 5: 1-12

It came to pass on the third day, Esther put on her royal dress and stood in the inner court of the king's house. When the king saw her, she obtained favor in his sight, and he called for her. He said, "What is your request, Queen Esther? It shall be even given thee to the half of the kingdom." She said, "If it is good for the king, let the king and Haman come this day to the banquet I have prepared for him." The king said, "Cause Haman to make haste that he may do as Esther hath said." So they came. The king said to Esther, "What is thy petition? It shall be granted thee." Esther answered, "My petition and my request is to let the king and Haman come to the banquet I have prepared for thee again tomorrow." Then Haman went forth with a joyful and glad heart. But when Haman saw Mordecai in the king's gate and he stood up not, nor moved for him, he was full of hate for Mordecai. Haman refrained himself. When he got home, he called for his friends and Zeresh his wife. He told them of the glory of his riches, and the king had promoted him. He said, "Esther, the queen, did not let anyone come in with the king unto the banquet she had prepared but myself; and tomorrow I am invited unto also with the king."

Haman's Evil Plan
Esther 5: 13-14

"Yet all this availeth me nothing as long as I see Mordecai the Jew sitting at the king's gate." Then said his wife and all his friends, "Let a gallows be made and tomorrow speak to the king that Mordecai may be hanged there." This pleased Haman

Deeds of Mordecai Made Known
Esther 6: 1-11

The king couldn't sleep, and he wanted to see the book of records. It was found written that Mordecai had told that he heard two of the king's chamberlains, the keepers of the door, that they wanted to kill the king. He said, "What honor and dignity hath been done to Mordecai for this? For saving my life?" Now Haman had come to speak to the king, to hang Mordecai. The king said, "Who is in the court?" The servants said, "Behold, Haman standeth in the court." The king said,

"Let him come in." Haman came in, and the king said, "What shall be done to the man I am delighted to honor?" Haman thought the king was talking about him. He said, "Let the royal apparel be brought and the horse the king rideth upon, and the crown royal be set upon his head." Then the king told Haman to take all the things and do even so to Mordecai the Jew, that sitteth at the gate. Haman did as he was told.

Haman Tells His Wife
Esther 6:13-14

Haman told his wife all that had happened. And while they were talking, the king's chamberlains came to bring Haman to the banquet that Esther had prepared.

Esther's Banquet
Esther 7: 1-8

The king told Esther she could have whatever she desired. "O King, my people are sold, and I and my people are to be destroyed, to be slain and perish. I had held my tongue." King Ahasuerus said, "Who is he, and where is he?" Esther said, "The adversary and enemy is this wicked Haman." Haman was afraid. The king went out to the palace garden. Haman stood up to make a request for his life to Esther because he saw there was evil determined against him by the king. When the king returned, Haman had fallen upon the bed where Esther was. He said, "Will he force the queen also?"

Haman's Fate
Esther 7:9-10

Haman was hanged on the gallows he had prepared for Mordecai.

Esther Pleads for Her People
Esther 8

Esther told the king that day what Mordecai was to her. The king gave him the ring he had taken from Haman. Esther said, "Please," and she fell down at his feet, and cried, "put away the mischief of Haman. If I have found favor in your sight, let it be written to reverse the letter devised by Haman." He gave Esther the house of Haman, and him they hanged on the gallows, because he laid his hand upon the Jews. So, the decree was given out to save the Jews—Do them no harm.

Mordecai Becomes Great
Esther 10

Mordecai the Jew was next unto king Ahasuerus, and great among the Jews and accepted of the brethren.

Chapter 5

Lesson 1
The New Testament Gospels
Matthew and Luke

We have finished our study in the Old Testament and it's been a journey. God's people are waiting for the Messiah. So, 400 years have passed and in those 400 years, the Greeks conquered God's promised land and the Romans conquered the Mediterranean world. Caesar Augustus rules the Roman Empire. As we start the New Testament, we will study about the birth and life of our Precious Savior Jesus Christ!!!

The Bloodline of Christ
Matthew 1: 1-17

Joseph is Jesus' legal father and Mary is his actual parent. Mary and Joseph were distant cousins. Read Matthew 1:1-16 to see the genealogy of Christ.

Joseph
Matthew 1:16

And Jacob begat (fathered) Joseph the husband of Mary, of whom was born Jesus, who is called Christ. Joseph was legally, but not physically, the father of Jesus. He was a carpenter of Nazareth, a legal heir of King David. Joseph was a God-fearing man, a carpenter of Nazareth, and a legal heir of King David.

Mary

Mary was a young Jewish girl betrothed to Joseph. Mary was a godly woman. An angel came to her and told her she would have a child and His name shall be called Jesus.

Jesus Was Born
Matthew 1: 18-25

Mary was espoused to Joseph, but before they came together, she was found with child of the Holy Ghost. Joseph, her husband, was a just man. He didn't want to make her a public example and was going to put her away privily (secretly). But an angel of the LORD appeared to him in a dream saying, "Joseph, thou Son of David, fear not to take Mary for your wife. For that which is conceived in her is of the Holy Ghost. She shall have a son and his name shall be JESUS, for he shall save his people from their sins." Now all this was done, it was spoken of the LORD by the prophet saying, "Behold, a virgin shall be with child, and shall bring forth a son, and his name shall be Emmanuel, which being interpreted is, God with us." Joseph awoke and did as the angel of the LORD had said. He took his wife. He knew her not until she brought forth her first born son: JESUS.

Micah 5:2

But thou, Bethlehem Ephrathah, though thou be little among the thousands of Judah, yet out of thee shall he come forth unto me that is to be ruler in Israel; whose goings forth have been from of old, from everlasting.

The Wise Men Visit Jesus
Matthew 2: 1-12

Jesus was born in Bethlehem of Judea in the days of Herod the king. Three wise men came to worship Jesus. They followed the star in the east. They asked, "Where is he that is born King of the Jews?" When King Herod heard all these things, he was troubled, and demanded where Christ should be born. They said, "In Bethlehem for it was written by the prophet." King Herod secretly called the wise men and asked diligently, "What time did the star appear?" He sent them to Bethlehem and said, "When you have found him, bring me word, that I may go and worship him also." They departed and followed the star in the east. It came and stood over where the young child was. They rejoiced when they saw the star. When they came into the house, they saw the young child with Mary, his mother, and they fell down and worshiped him. They gave him gifts of gold, frankincense, and myrrh. They were warned in a dream from God, "DO NOT return to Herod; go home another way."

Journey to Egypt
Matthew 2: 13-18

When they departed, the angel of the LORD appeared to Joseph in a dream to take the young child and his mother and flee to Egypt. "Stay until I bring you word. Herod will seek the child to destroy him." Joseph took them by night. They stayed until the death of Herod. But, when Herod saw he was mocked by the wise men, he was wroth (angry) and sent forth and slew all the children from 2 years old and under.

Joseph is Warned in a Dream
Matthew 2: 19-23

When Herod died, an angel of the LORD appeared to Joseph in a dream saying, "Take the young child and his mother and go into the land of Israel for they are dead that sought to kill the young child." But when he heard that Herod's son, Archelaus was king, who was more evil than his father, he was afraid to go. Being warned by God in a dream, he turned into parts of Galilee and dwelt in Nazareth; that it might be fulfilled which was spoken by the prophet, He shall be called a Nazarene.

Isaiah 7:14

Therefore, the LORD himself shall give you a sign, behold, a virgin shall conceive, and bear a son and shall call his name Immanuel.

Isaiah 9:6

For unto us a child is born, unto us a son is given; and the government shall be upon his shoulder, and his name shall be called Wonderful, Counselor, The mighty God, The Everlasting Father, The Prince of Peace.

John the Baptist

Zacharias and Elizabeth are the parents of John The Baptist. They had prayed for a child but Elizabeth had been barren. Elizabeth was six months pregnant when the angel came to Mary, Elizabeth's cousin, and told her she would have a son and His name would be Jesus. John the Baptist was the forerunner of Jesus and filled with the Holy Spirit from his birth. John lived in the wilderness, wore clothes made of camel's hair, and a leather belt around his waist. He ate locust and wild honey. He went about preaching repentance. Herod Antipas had John beheaded. (Matthew 14) John did not understand that Jesus was the Son of God until he baptized Jesus and witnessed God's supernatural witness of Jesus' baptism. Jesus declared among them that are born of women, there hath not risen a greater man than John the Baptist. (Matthew 11:11)

The Angel Gabriel Comes to Mary
Luke 1: 26

And in the sixth month, the angel Gabriel was sent from God unto a city of Galilee named Nazareth to a virgin espoused to a man whose name was Joseph, of the house of David; and the virgin's name was Mary. The angel came to her and told her she was highly favored, "The LORD is with thee; blessed are thou among women." When Mary saw him, she was troubled at what he was saying. The angel said, "Fear not, Mary for thou hast found favor with God. And behold, thou shalt conceive in thy womb, and bring forth a son, and shall call his name JESUS." Mary said unto the angel, "How shall this be, seeing I know not a man?" The angel answered and said, "The Holy Ghost shall come upon thee, and the power of the Highest shall overshadow thee. Therefore, also that holy thing which shall be born of thee shall be called the Son of God. And behold, thy cousin Elizabeth, hath also conceived a son in her old age. And this is the sixth month with her, who was called barren. With God nothing shall be impossible." And Mary said, "Behold the handmaid of the LORD; be it unto me according to thy word." And the angel departed from her.

Elizabeth and Mary
Luke 1: 39-45

Mary arose and went into the hill country, into the city of Judea, and entered into the house of Zacharias and saluted Elizabeth. When Elizabeth heard the salutation of Mary, the babe leapt in her womb, and she was filled with the Holy Ghost. She spoke with a loud voice, "Blessed art thou among women, and blessed is the fruit of thy womb. And whence is this to me, that the mother of my LORD should come to me? For as soon as the voice of thy salutation sounded in mine ears, the babe leapt in my womb for joy."

Jesus Born in Bethlehem
Luke 2: 1-9

Caesar Augustus put out a decree that all the world should be taxed. Joseph went up from Nazareth to Bethlehem, the city of David because he was of the house and lineage of David to be taxed with Mary his espoused wife, being great with child. While they were there, the days were accomplished that she should deliver. She brought forth her firstborn son, and wrapped him in swaddling clothes, and laid him in a manger, because there was no room in the inn.

***In Matthew, the Bible speaks about the wise men following the star in the east to find Jesus. They called Him, "King of the Jews." Herod wanted the wise men to tell him where this child is. And God told them not to go back to Herod, to go home a different way. Herod became very angry and had the children 2 years and younger killed. God told Joseph in a dream about the evil of Herod. So he and Mary took the child, Jesus, and fled to Egypt. And returned to Israel after Herod's death.

Hosea 11:1

When Israel was a child, then I loved him, and called my son out of Egypt.

***Even before God sent His only son, the prophet told of His coming. It is amazing how God spoke to these men and they foretold the future. Hosea was one of these men that God used.

Luke

Luke, a Gentile, was a physician. (Colossians 4:14) Paul taught Luke the gospel as he traveled with Paul.

Luke 3: 38

Luke traces Jesus' lineage all the way back to Adam, The Son of God.

Jesus About His Father's Business
Luke 2: 39-52

Jesus' parents went to Jerusalem every year at the feast of the Passover. Jesus grew and was strong in spirit, filled with wisdom and the grace of God was upon Him. When He was 12 years old, they went to Jerusalem. When they had fulfilled the days, and as they returned, the child tarried behind. Joseph and Mary, His mother, did not know it. They went a day's journey, and they looked for him among their family and friends. When they didn't find him, they went back to Jerusalem looking for him. After 3 days, they found Him in the temple, sitting in the midst of the doctors, both hearing them and asking questions. They were all astonished at his understanding and answers. When Joseph and Mary saw Him they were amazed. His mother said, "Son, why hast thou thus dwelt with us? Behold, thy father and I have sought thee sorrowing." And He said, "<u>How is it that ye sought me? Wist ye not that I must be about my Father's Business?</u>" And He went down with them, back to Nazareth, and was subject unto them. But His mother kept all these sayings in her heart. Jesus increased in wisdom and stature, and in favor with God and man.

Lesson 2

<u>The Life of Jesus Continues</u>
Matthew 3: 1-12

John was preaching in the wilderness saying, "Repent ye, for the kingdom of heaven is at hand." This is He that was spoken of by the prophet Esaias saying, "The voice of one crying in the wilderness." John wore his raiment of camel's hair, a leather girdle about his lions, and his meat was locusts and wild honey. They came from Jerusalem and all Judea, and around Jordan, and baptized in the Jordan, confessing their sins. He said, "I indeed baptize you with water unto repentance, but he that cometh after me is mightier than I, whose shoes I am not worthy to bear. He shall baptize you with the Holy Ghost, and with fire whose fan is in his hand, and he will thoroughly purge his floor, and gather his wheat into the garner; but he will burn up the chaff with unquenchable fire."

***The unquenchable fire refers to the eternal punishment of hell or the lake of fire.

Jesus Baptized
Matthew 3: 13-17

Jesus came from Galilee to Jordan to be baptized by John the Baptist. John forbade him, saying, "I have need to be baptized of you, and you come to me?" Jesus said, "Suffer it to be done now for thus it becometh us to fulfill all righteousness." Then John baptized him. Then Jesus went straightway out of the water, the heavens opened unto him, he saw the Spirit of God descending like a dove, and lighting upon Him; and lo, a voice from heaven saying, "This is my beloved Son, in whom I am well pleased."

Jesus Tempted
Matthew 4: 1-11

The Spirit led Jesus in the wilderness to be tempted by the devil. He fasted 40 days and 40 nights and was hungry. The tempter (devil) said, "If you are the Son of God, command these stones to turn to bread." Jesus answered, "It is written, man shall not live by bread alone, but by every word that proceedeth out of the mouth of God." Then the devil took him unto the holy city and set him on the pinnacle of the temple. The devil said, "If you are the Son of God, cast thyself down." Jesus said, "It is written again, thou shalt not tempt the LORD thy God." Then the devil took him upon an exceedingly high mountain, and showed him all the kingdoms of the world, and the glory of them. He said, "All this I give thee, if you will fall down and worship me." Then Jesus said, "Get thee hence, Satan: for it is written, Thou shalt worship the LORD thy God, and him only shalt thou serve." Then the devil left him, and the angels came and ministered unto him.

Ministry of Jesus
Matthew 4: 12-17

Jesus departed into Galilee when he heard that John the Baptist was in prison. When Jesus left Nazareth, he dwelt in Capernaum.

***This is where Matthew first met Jesus. (Matthew 9:9) Esaias the prophet said that it might be fulfilled. (Matthew 4:14)

***Refers to the coming of Jesus Christ into Galilee in fulfillment of the prophecy of Isaiah 9: 1-2 Beyond Jordan, in Galilee of the nations. The people that walked in darkness have seen a great light.

***Jesus said, "I am the light of the world: he that followeth me shall not walk in darkness but shall have the light of life." (John 8:12)

***Jesus performed most of His miracles in Capernaum. Reading about the many miracles: (Luke 5:1-11) the miraculous catch of fish, (Matthew 8:14-15) Peter's mother-in-law healed, (Mark 2: 1-12) the friends of a paralytic man took the roof off to lower him in the house to be healed, (Mark 5:25-34) the woman healed from bleeding for 12 years, (Luke 8:40-56) the little sick girl that died and Jesus brought her back to life. There were several more miracles Jesus performed and the people still would not repent.

The 12 Disciples of Jesus
Luke 6:12-16

Jesus chose 12 apostles who would learn from him and assist him in his mission. Simon (whom he named Peter), his brother Andrew, James, John, Philip, Bartholomew, Matthew, Thomas, James the son of Alphaeus, Simon who was called the Zealot, Judas brother of James, and Judas Iscariot, who became a traitor. He betrayed Jesus for 30 pieces of silver, and afterwards hanged himself.

*** How could anyone so close to Jesus betray him? He was the treasurer. Judas did betray Jesus, but it was our sin that put Jesus on the cross.

Jesus Calls the First Four Disciples
Matthew 4: 18-22

Jesus was walking by the Sea of Galilee. He saw Simon Peter and his brother Andrew casting a net into the sea. They were fishermen. Jesus told them, "Follow me and I will make you fishers of men." They left their nets and followed JESUS. As they were going, Jesus saw James and John, the sons of Zebedee mending their nets and he called them. They immediately left the ship and their father and followed JESUS.

Just a Little Info on the First Four Disciples

Simon Peter- He was one of the 12 disciples of Jesus Christ. He was a fisherman. He received the name Cephas meaning stone (rock) (John 1:42). Peter was listed first among the 12. Peter's faith allowed him to walk on water until he took his eyes off the LORD. (Matthew 14:28-30) He denied Jesus three times. (Matthew 26) Peter was crucified at Rome with his head downwards.

Andrew- He was the brother to Peter. Also, one of the first 4 apostles of the 12. He was a fisherman like his brother Peter. Andrew was the first to refer to Jesus as the Messiah. (John 1:41)

James, The Son of Zebedee- James is also the brother of Simon Peter and Andrew as well as a fisherman. (Matthew 4:18-19) Peter, James, and John witnessed the raising of Jairus' daughter. (Mark 5:37-39) Herod the King killed him with the sword. (Acts 12:1-3)

John, the Fourth Disciple- John, son of Zebedee, was brother to James. John lived a long life and was the last remaining disciple. He wrote the fourth gospel, his three epistles (letters), and Revelation. John was at Jesus' crucifixion. John was always loyal to Jesus. Before Jesus died he told John to watch over his mother Mary who was also present at the crucifixion. The Romans put John on Patmos for preaching God's word. (Revelation 1:9) Patmos was a small, rocky, and barren area. The Romans sent many criminals to Patmos to serve out their prison terms as they were harsh conditions. While John was on Patmos, he began to have visions that were written into the book of Revelation. John was the one disciple that died of natural causes.

Jesus Teaching and Healing
Matthew 4: 23-25

Jesus went all about Galilee teaching in their synagogues and preaching the gospel of the kingdom, healing the sick and people with disease. Jesus became famous throughout all Syria. They brought all sick people with divers diseases and tormented. Some were possessed with devils and lunatics, some had palsy; He healed them all. Great multitudes of people followed Jesus. He went from city to city throughout Galilee.

Matthew 7: 12

Therefore, all things whatsoever ye would that men should do to you, do ye even so to them: for this is the law and the prophets.

Matthew 10: 1

Jesus gave the apostles power against unclean spirits, to cast them out, and to heal all manner of sickness and all manner of diseases.

Matthew 10: 5-6

Jesus sent the 12 forth and commanded them, "<u>Go not into the way of the Gentiles, and into any city of the Samaritans. But go to the lost sheep of the house of Israel._</u>"

***The children of Israel are God's chosen people, and he wants them to repent and return to Him.

Jesus Talking to His Disciples
Matthew 13: 18-23

Jesus went out of the house and was sitting by the sea. Multitudes gathered unto Him and Jesus went into the ship and the multitude stood by the shore. He spoke to them in parables saying, "Behold, a sower went forth to sow. The seed is spread throughout the world. Some fall by the wayside; the fowls devoured them. Some fell in stony place, not much earth; so when they sprung up, they had no earth and the sun dried them up because they had no roots. Some fell in thorns; the thorns sprung up and choked them. Some fell on good ground and brought forth fruit, some a hundredfold, some sixty fold, some thirty fold. Who hath ears to hear. Unsaved people do not understand and do not receive the seed." The disciples asked, "Why do you speak in parables?" Jesus answered, "You know the mysteries of the kingdom of heaven but to them, it is not given. The ones that hear and don't understand it. Then comes the wicked one and takes away that was sown in his heart and the seed falls by the wayside. The same is the seed planted in stony places, he has not rooted himself. He that received seed among the thorns hears the word, but the word is choked out and he becomes unfruitful. But he that received good seed into the ground, he heareth the word, understands, and bringeth forth some hundred fold, some sixty, some thirty. All true believers will produce some fruit."

The Disciples Are Prepared by Jesus
Matthew 16:20-28

Jesus tells them how he must go to Jerusalem and suffer many things of the elders, chief priests, and scribes, and be killed and raised again the third day. It was hard for his disciples to understand that Jesus would be killed.

*** They didn't look at things from God's point of view, but from man's.

Matthew 21: 9

And the multitudes that went before and that followed cried saying, "Hosanna to the Son of David. Blessed is he that cometh in the name of the LORD. Hosanna in the highest."

Lesson 3

Garden of Gethsemane

Gethsemane is the place where Jesus prayed before His crucifixion where He asked His disciples to pray and they fell asleep. Jesus asked His father to take this cup from Him; nevertheless, not what I will, but what Thou wilt. He was betrayed by Judas and was arrested. Jesus had become famous from His preaching and He had healed the sick. The Pharisees, the Scribes, and the Sadducees didn't like Jesus.

Sadducees: They didn't believe in the resurrection. (Matthew 22:23) Jesus' claim to be one with God made the Sadducees believe there was a threat to their authority in the Temple.

Scribes: Jesus was angry when He went into the temple and He saw that there was selling and buying there. He overthrew the money changers and the seats of them that sold doves. He said, "Is it not written, my house shall be called of all nations the house of prayer? But ye have made it a den of thieves." The Scribes were lawyers. They feared Jesus because all the people were astonished at His doctrine. They wanted to destroy Jesus.

<u>Pharisees:</u> They followed the Jewish law. They were lawyers and had heard He had put the Sadducees to silence, they gathered together. One asked Him a question, tempting Him, "Master, which is greatest commandment in the law?" Jesus answered, "Thou shalt love the LORD thy God with all they heart, soul, and all thy mind." As Jesus talked to them, no man was able to answer Him a word, and they asked Him no more questions.

<u>The Plan to Kill Jesus</u>
Matthew 26: 1-5

After Jesus had finished His sayings, He said to his disciples, "<u>Ye know after two days is the feast of the Passover, and the Son of Man is betrayed to be crucified.</u>" The chief priest, the scribes, and elders of the people came to the palace of the high priest. They consulted that they might take Jesus by subtilty and kill him. But not on the feast day, because there might be an uproar.

<u>Alabaster Box of Ointment</u>
Matthew 26: 6-13

Jesus was in Bethany, in the house of Simon the leper. A woman came with an alabaster box of very precious ointment and poured it on His (Jesus') head. When his disciples saw it, they said, "To what purpose is this waste? For this ointment might have been sold for much and given to the poor." When Jesus understood it, He said, "Why trouble ye the woman? For she hath done a good work upon me. You have the poor with you always, but I will not be with you always. For in that she poured this ointment on my body, she did it for my burial. Whosoever this gospel shall be preached in the whole world, there shall also this be told, for a memorial of her."

Judas Iscariot Betrays Jesus
Matthew 26: 14-16

Then one of the 12, Judas Iscariot went to the chief priest, and said, "What will you give me if I will deliver Jesus unto you?" They said, "30 pieces of silver." Then he sought opportunity to betray Jesus.

Passover Meal
Matthew 26: 17-30

Now the first day of the feast of unleavened bread, the disciples came to Jesus and asked, "Where wilt thou that we prepare to eat the Passover meal?" He said, "Go into the city to such a man, and say to him, 'The master saith my time is at hand. I will keep the Passover at thy house with my disciples.'" The disciples went and made ready the Passover. When the even came, He sat down with the 12 and they did eat. Jesus said, "Verily I say unto you, that one of you shall betray me." They were exceedingly sorrowful, and began to question and said unto him, "LORD, is it I?" He answered and said, "He that dippeth his hand with me in the dish, it is he. The Son of man goeth as it is written of him, but woe unto that man by whom the Son of man is betrayed! It would have been good that he had not been born." Judas answered and said, "Master, is it I?" Jesus said, "Thou hast said." As they were eating, Jesus took bread, blessed it, and brake it, and gave it to the disciples and said, "Take, eat; this is my body." He took the cup, and gave thanks, and gave it to them saying, "Drink ye all of it; for this is my blood of the New Testament, which is shed for many for the remission of sins. But I say unto you, I will not drink henceforth of this fruit of the vine until that day when I drink it new with you in my Father's kingdom." When they had sung a hymn, they went into the mount of Olives.

Peter Makes a Vow to Jesus
Matthew 26: 31-35

Then saith Jesus, "All ye shall be offended because of me this night. For it is written, 'I will smite the shepherd, and the sheep of the flock shall be scattered abroad.' But after I am risen again, I will go before you into Galilee." Peter answered and said, "Though all men shall be offended because of thee, I will never be offended." Jesus said to him, "Verily I say unto thee, that this night, before the cock crow, thou shalt deny me thrice (3 times)." Peter said, "Though I should die with thee, yet will I not deny thee." The others said the same.

Jesus Prays in Gethsemane
Matthew 26: 36-46

Then Jesus went unto Gethsemane and saith unto his disciples, "Sit here while I go and pray yonder." He took with him Peter and the two sons of Zebedee and began to be sorrowful and very heavy. He said to them, "My soul is exceeding sorrowful, even unto death: tarry ye here, and watch with me." He went a little farther, and fell on his face, and prayed saying, "O my Father, if it be possible, let this cup pass from Me; nevertheless, not as I will, but as Thou wilt." He then came unto the disciples, and found them asleep, and saith unto Peter, "What, could ye not watch with me one hour? Watch and pray, that ye enter not into temptation. The spirit indeed is willing, but the flesh is weak." He went away again the second time, and prayed saying, "O my Father, if this cup may not pass away from Me, except I drink it, Thy will be done." Jesus came and found them asleep again for their eyes were heavy. He left them, and went away again, and prayed the third time saying the same words. Then he came to His disciples, and saith unto them, "Sleep on now, and take your rest. Behold, the hour is at hand, and the Son of man is betrayed into the hands of sinners. Rise, let us be going; behold, he is at hand that doth betray Me."

Jesus Betrayed
Matthew 26: 47-56

And while He spake, lo, Judas came, and with him a great multitude with swords and staves from the chief priest and elders of the people. Judas gave them a sign saying, "Whomsoever I shall kiss, that same is he. Hold him fast." And he came to Jesus, and said, "Hail, Master; and kissed him." Jesus said unto him, "Friend, wherefore art thou come?" Then they came, laid hands on Jesus, and took him. And behold, one of them which were with Jesus stretched out his hand, and drew his sword, and struck a servant of the high priests, and cut off his ear. Then Jesus said, "Put up thy sword, for all they that take the sword shall perish with the sword. Thinkest thou that I cannot pray to My Father, and He shall presently give Me more than twelve legions of angels? But how then shall the scriptures be fulfilled, that thus it must be?" In that same hour, Jesus said to the multitudes, "Are ye come out as against a thief with sword and staves for to take me? I sat daily with you teaching in the temple, and ye laid no hold on me. But all this was done that the scriptures of the prophets might be fulfilled." Then all the disciples forsook him and fled.

***He was being accused of blasphemy and the punishment was to be put to death.

Luke 22:50 And one of them smote the servant of the high priest and cut off his right ear.

Caiaphas the High Priest
Matthew 26: 57-68

They took Jesus to Caiaphas the high priest where the scribes and the elders were assembled. Peter followed afar off unto the high priest's palace, and went in, and sat with the servant, to see the end. They all sought false witness against Jesus, to put him to death, but found none; yea, though many false witnesses came, yet found they none. At the last came two false witnesses, and said, "This fellow said He is able to destroy the temple of God and build it again in three days." The high priest arose, and said unto him, "Answerest thou nothing? What is it, which these witness against thee?" But Jesus held his peace, and the high priest answered and said to him, "I adjure thee by the living God, that thou tell us whether thou be the Christ, the Son of God." Jesus said, "Thou hast said; nevertheless, I say unto you, hereafter shall ye see the Son of man sitting on the right hand of power and coming in the clouds of heaven." Then the high priest rent his clothes saying, "He hath spoken blasphemy; what further need have we of witnesses? Behold, ye have not heard his blasphemy. What think ye?" They answered and said, "He is guilty of death." They did spit in his face, and buffeted (hit) him; and others smote him with the palms of their hands saying, "Prophesy unto us, thou Christ, who is he that smote thee?"

Peter's Denial
Matthew 26: 69-75

Peter sat without in the palace. A damsel came and said, "Thou also wast with Jesus of Galilee." Peter denied before them all saying, "I know not what thou sayest." When he went out to the porch, another maid saw him and said, "This fellow was also with Jesus of Nazareth." And again he denied with an oath, "I do not know the man." And after a while, came unto him they that stood by and said to Peter, "Surely you are one of them for thy speech betrayeth thee." Then Peter began to curse and swear, saying, "I know not the man." And immediately the cock crowed. And Peter remembered the word of Jesus, "Before the cock crow, thou shalt deny me thrice." And he went out and wept bitterly.

Judas Has Remorse
Matthew 27: 1-10

When the morning came, they took counsel against Jesus to put him to death. They bound him, led him away, and delivered him to Pontius Pilate the governor. When Judas saw that Jesus was condemned, he repented himself, and brought the 30 pieces of silver to the chief priest and elders saying, "I have sinned in that I have betrayed the innocent blood." And they said, "What is that to us? See thou to that."

And he cast down the pieces of silver in the temple and departed and went and hanged himself. The chief priest took the silver pieces and said, "It is not lawful for to put them into the treasure because it is the price of blood." And they took counsel, and bought with them the potter's field, to bury strangers in. Wherefore that field was called the field of blood unto this day. Then was fulfilled that which was spoken by Jeremiah the prophet saying, "And they took the 30 pieces of silver, the price of Him that was valued, whom they of the children of Israel did value, and gave them for the potter's field, as the LORD appointed me.

<u>Jesus Stands Before Pilate</u>
Matthew 27: 11-26

Jesus stood before the governor. He asked Jesus saying, "Art thou the King of the Jews?" And Jesus said to him, "<u>Thou sayest.</u>" When he was accused of them, He said nothing. Then Pilate said, "Hearest thou not how many things they witness against thee?" Jesus never said a word and the governor marveled greatly. At the feast, the governor was to release unto the people a prisoner, whom they chose. They had a notable prisoner called Barabbas. Pilate said unto them, "Whom will ye that I release unto you, Barabbas or Jesus which is called Christ?" For he knew that for envy they had delivered him. When he sat down on the judgment seat, his wife sent to him saying, "Have thou nothing to do with that just man, for I have suffered many things this day in a dream because of him." But the chief priest and elders persuaded the multitude that they should ask for Barabbas and destroy Jesus. The governor answered and said unto them, "Whether of the two will ye that I release unto you?" They said, "Barabbas." Pilate said unto them, "What shall I do then with

Jesus?" They all said, "Let Him be crucified." The governor said, "Why, what evil hath he done?" But they cried the more saying, "Let Him be crucified." When Pilate saw that he could not stop them, he took water, and washed his hands before the multitude saying, "I am innocent of the blood of this just person. See ye to it." They said, "His blood be on us, and our children." They released Barabbas to them. And when he had scourged Jesus, he delivered him to be crucified.
*** Barabbas was a murderer (Mark 15:7) and a robber (John 18:40).

Jesus Scourged
Mathew 27: 27-31

The soldiers took Jesus into the common hall, stripped Him, and put a scarlet robe on Him. They plaited a crown of thorns, and put on His head, a reed in His right hand. They bowed the knee before Him, and mocked Him saying, "Hail, King of the Jews." They spit on Him, and took the reed, and smote Him on the head. And after they had mocked Him, they took the robe off Him, and put His own raiment on Him, and led Him away to crucify Him.

Pilate Finds No Fault
Luke 23: 1-6

The whole multitude rose and led Him to Pilate. They began to accuse Him saying, "We found this fellow perverting the nation, and forbidding to give tribute to Caesar saying that He Himself is Christ the king." Pilate asked, "Art thou the King of the Jews?" Jesus answered, "Thou sayest it." Then Pilate said to the chief priests and to the people, "I find no fault in this man." They became more fierce saying, "He stirreth up the people, teaching throughout all Jewry (Jewish people), beginning from Galilee to this place." When Pilate heard of Galilee, he asked whether the man was a Galilean.

*** Trying to pass the buck here!!

From Pilate to Herod
Luke 23: 7-12

When he realized He belonged in Herod's jurisdiction, he sent Him to Herod. When Herod saw Jesus, He was exceedingly glad. He was desirous to see him of a long season because he had heard many things of him and hoped to have seen some miracle done by him. He questioned Jesus, but Jesus answered nothing. The chief priest and scribes stood and strongly accused him. Herod, with his men of war, set him at nought, mocked him, and arrayed him in a gorgeous robe, and sent him again to Pilate. And the same day Pilate and Herod made friends together, for before they were enemies.

Pilate Sees No Fault in Jesus
Luke 23: 13-25

Pilate called the chief priest and rulers of the people and said unto them, "I find no fault in this Man touching those things where of ye accuse Him. No, nor ye Herod. For I sent You to him; and lo, nothing worthy of death is done unto Him. I will therefore chastise Him and release Him. (For of necessity he must release one unto them at the feast.)" And they cried out all at once saying, "Away with this Man, and release unto us Barabbas (who for a certain sedition made in the city, and for murder, was cast into prison.) Pilate, therefore, willing to release Jesus, spake again to them. But they cried saying, "Crucify Him, crucify Him." And he said unto them the third time, "Why? What evil hath he done? I have found no cause of death in him. I will therefore chastise Him and let Him go." And they were instant with a loud voice, requiring that he might be crucified. And the voices of them and the chief priest prevailed. And he released unto them Barabbas that for sedition and murder was cast into prison, whom they had desired; but he delivered Jesus to their will.

Lesson 4
The Crucifixion and Resurrection of Our Lord Jesus Christ

Pilate was really in disbelief that the people could hate Jesus so much and wanted to free a murderer, Barabbas. The people continually yelled to crucify Jesus.

Luke 23:23 And they were instant with loud voices, requiring that he might be crucified. And the voices of them and of the chief priests prevailed.
***Jesus had told His disciples that He would be betrayed by one of their own. That He would be mocked, scourged, and crucified. And would rise the third day. Pilate knew Jesus was falsely accused, he still let the people take him. When Jesus was hanged, they put a sign over Him with the words, KING OF THE JEWS.

Jesus Tortured and Mocked
John 19: 1-16

Pilate took Jesus and scourged him. The soldiers platted a crown of thorns, put it on his head, and put a purple robe on him. And said, "Hail, King of the Jews!" And they smote him with their hands. Pilate went forth again and said, "Behold, I bring Him forth to you, that ye may know that I find no fault in Him." Then Jesus came forth and Pilate said, "Behold the Man!" When the chief priest and officers saw him, they cried out saying, "Crucify Him, crucify Him." Pilate said, "Take Him and crucify Him for I find no fault in Him." The Jews answered him, "We have a law, and by our law He ought to die because He made Himself the Son of God." When Pilate heard that, he was more afraid. He went again into the judgment hall and said to Jesus, "Whence art thou?" But Jesus gave him no answer. Pilate said, "Well, don't speak to me. Do you not know I have power to crucify Thee, and have power to release Thee?" Jesus answered, "Thou couldest have no power at all against Me, except it were given thee from above; therefore, he that delivered Me unto thee hath the greater sin." And from then, Pilate wanted to release Him but the Jews cried out saying, "If thou let this Man go, thou art not Caesar's friend. Whoever maketh himself a king, speaketh against Caesar." When Pilate heard that saying, he brought Jesus forth, and sat down in the judgment seat in a place that is called the Pavement, but in the Hebrew, Gabbatha. It was the preparation of the Passover, and about the sixth hour and he said to the Jews, "Behold your king!" But they cried out, "Away with Him, away with Him, crucify Him." Pilate said, "Shall I crucify your King?" The chief priest answered, "We have no king but Caesar. Deliver him therefore to be crucified." And they took Jesus and led him away.

On The Hill of Golgotha
John 19: 17-27

And He, bearing his cross, went forth into a place called the place of a skull, which is called in the Hebrew Golgotha where they crucified Him, and two others with Him, one on either side, and Jesus in the midst. Pilate wrote a title and put it on the cross. JESUS OF NAZARETH THE KING OF THE JEWS. The chief priests of the Jews said to Pilate, "Write not The King of the Jews but what He said, 'I am King of the Jews.'" Pilate said, "What I have written I have written." Then the soldiers, when they had crucified Jesus, took his garments and made four parts, to every soldier a part, and also his coat. Now the coat was without seam, woven from the top throughout. "Let us cast lots for the coat, whose it shall be." They parted my raiment among them, and for my vesture they did cast lots. Standing by the cross was his mother, Mary, and his mother's sister, Mary the wife of Cleophas, and Mary Magdalene. When Jesus saw his mother and the disciple standing by whom he loved, He said unto his mother, "Woman, behold thy son!" Then saith He to the disciple, "Behold thy mother!" And from that hour, that disciple took her unto his own home.

***John was the disciple.

Luke 23:34

Then Jesus said, "Father, forgive them; for they know not what they do." And they parted his raiment and cast lots.

Luke 23: 39-43

One of the men hanging on the cross with Jesus said, "If thou be Christ, save Thyself and us." But the other rebuked him saying, "Dost not thou fear God, seeing thou art in the same condemnation? And we indeed justly; for we received the due reward of our deeds: but this Man hath done nothing amiss." He said to Jesus, "Lord, remember me when thou comest into thy kingdom." And Jesus said, "<u>Verily I say unto thee, today shalt thou be with Me in paradise.</u>"

*** Mary Magdalene was one of the followers of Jesus. Jesus cleansed her of seven demons. (Luke 8:2) She was with other Mary's at the crucifixion and burial of Jesus. These women were the first to see Jesus after the resurrection.

Jesus on the Old Rugged Cross
Matthew 27: 45-56

Now from the sixth hour, there was darkness over all the land unto the ninth hour. About the ninth hour, Jesus cried with a loud voice saying, "<u>Eli, Eli, lama Sabathani?</u>" That is to say, <u>My God, my God, why hast thou forsaken me?</u> Some said, "This Man calleth Elias." And straightway one of them ran and took a sponge, and filled it with vinegar, and put it on a reed, and gave Him to drink. The rest said, "Let be, let us see whether Elias will come to save him." Jesus, when he had cried again with a loud voice, yielded up the ghost, and behold, the veil of the temple was rent in twain from the top to the bottom and the earth did quake, and the rocks rent, graves opened, and many bodies of the saints which slept arose and came out of the graves after His resurrection, and went into the holy city, and appeared unto many. The Centurion, and they that were with him watching Jesus, saw the earthquake, and those things that were done. They feared greatly saying, "Truly this was the Son the of God." Many women were there beholding afar off: Mary Magdalene, Mary the mother of James and Joses, and the mother of Zebedee's children.

Joseph Buries Jesus in His Own Tomb
Matthew 27: 57- 61

When the even came, a rich man named Joseph, also one of Jesus' disciples went to Pilate and begged for the body of Jesus. Joseph took the body. He wrapped it in a clean linen cloth and laid it in his own new tomb, which he had hewn out in the rock; and he rolled a great stone to the door of the sepulcher and departed. And there was Mary Magdalene, and the other Mary, sitting over against the sepulcher.

The Watch
Matthew 27: 62-66

The next day, the chief priest and Pharisees came together unto Pilate saying, "Sir, we remember what that deceiver said while he was yet alive: 'After three days I will rise again.' Command that the sepulcher be made sure until the third day, lest his disciples come by night, and steal him away, and say unto the people, 'He is risen from the dead.' So the last error shall be worse than the first." Pilate said, "Ye have a watch. Go your way, make it as sure as ye can." So they went, sealing the stone, and setting a watch.

Jesus Has Risen
Matthew 28: 1-15

In the end of the Sabbath, the first day of the week, came Mary Magdalene and the other Mary to see the sepulcher. And behold, there was a great earthquake for the angel of the LORD descended from heaven, came and rolled back the stone from the door, and sat upon it. His countenance was like lightning, and his raiment white as snow. And for fear of him, the keepers did shake, and became as dead men. The angel answered and said to the women, "Fear not ye for I know that ye seek Jesus, which was crucified. He is not here: for he is risen, as he said. Come, see the place where the LORD lay. And go quickly and tell His disciples that He is risen from the dead; and behold, He goeth before you into Galilee. There shall ye see Him. Lo, I have told you." They departed quickly from the sepulcher with fear and great joy; and did run to tell His disciples. And as they went to tell them, behold, Jesus met them saying, "All hail." And they came and held Him by the feet and worshiped Him. Jesus said, "Be not afraid; go tell my brethren that they go into Galilee, and there shall they see Me." Now when they were going, some of the watch came into the city, and shewed the chief priests all the things that were done. When they were assembled with the elders, and had taken counsel, they gave a large amount of money to the soldiers saying, "Say ye, 'His disciples came by night and stole Him away while we slept.' And if this come to the governor's ears, we will persuade him, and secure you." So they took the money and did as they were taught and this saying is commonly reported among the Jews until this day.

Jesus' Appearance to Eleven Disciples
Mark 16: 14-20

He appeared to eleven of His disciples as they sat at meat and upbraided them with their unbelief and hardness of heart because they believed not them which had seen Him after He was risen. Jesus said, "<u>Go ye into all the world, and preach the gospel to every creature. He that believeth and is baptized shall be saved; but he that believeth not shall be damned. And these signs shall follow them that believe: in My name shall they cast out devils; they shall speak with new tongues; they shall take up serpents; and if they drink any deadly thing, it shall not hurt them; they shall lay hands on the sick, and they shall recover."</u>

Doubting Thomas
John 20: 24-31

Thomas, one of the twelve, was not with them when Jesus came. The other disciples said, "We have seen the Lord." But he said, "Except I shall see in His hands the print of the nails and put my finger into the print of the nails, and thrust my hand into His side, I will not believe." And after eight days, again His disciples were within and Thomas with them. Then came Jesus, the doors being shut, and stood in the midst and said, "<u>Peace be unto you.</u>" Then He said to Thomas, "<u>Reach hither thy finger, and behold my hands; and reach hither thy hand and thrust it into my side: and be not faithless but believing.</u>" Thomas answered and said, "My Lord and my God." Jesus said, "<u>Thomas, because thou hast seen Me, thou hast believed; blessed are they that have not seen, and yet have believed.</u>" Many other signs truly did Jesus do in the presence of His disciples, which are not written in this book. But these are written, that ye might believe that Jesus is the

Christ, the Son of God and that believing ye might have life through His Name.

Jesus Blessed His Disciples and Ascended into Heaven
Luke 24: 50-53 and Acts 1:7-9

And he led them out as far as to Bethany, and He lifted up His hands and blessed them. And it came to pass, while He blessed them, He was parted from them, and carried up into heaven. And they worshiped Him and returned to Jerusalem with great joy. And were continually in the temple, praising and blessing God. Amen.

Lesson 5

Jesus Gives Direction to His Disciples
Matthew 28: 16-20

Then the eleven disciples went away into Galilee, into a mountain where Jesus had appointed them. And when they saw Him, they worshiped Him; but some doubted. And Jesus came and spake unto them saying, "All power is given unto me in heaven and in earth. Go ye therefore, and teach all nations, baptizing them in the name of the Father, and of the Son, and of the Holy Ghost; teaching them to observe all things whatsoever I have commanded you. And lo, I am with you always, even unto the end of the world." Amen.

Jesus Commanding the Eleven
Mark 16:14-18

Afterward he appeared to the eleven as they sat at meat and upbraided them with their unbelief and hardness of heart, because they believed not them which had seen him after he was risen. Jesus said, "<u>Go ye into all the world, and preach the gospel to every creature. He that believeth and is baptized shall be saved; but he that believeth not shall be damned. And these signs shall follow them that believe: in my name shall they cast our devils, they shall speak with new tongues, they shall take up serpents, and if they drink any deadly thing, it shall not hurt them, they shall lay hands on the sick and they shall recover.</u>

Forty Days

Jesus stayed 40 days on earth after His resurrection.

***Jesus wanted to get across to the disciples that after He leaves the earth, for them to preach the gospel to all, to be baptized, and to be saved.

<u>Acts 2: 1-4</u> And when the day of Pentecost was fully come, they were all with one accord in one place. And suddenly there came a sound from heaven as of a rushing mighty wind, it filled all the house where they were sitting. There appeared to them cloven tongues like as of fire, and it sat upon each of them. They were filled with the Holy Ghost; they began to speak in tongues, as the Spirit gave them utterance.

Pentecost
Acts 2:12-16, 21

***The Pentecost is celebrated on the seventh Sunday after Easter. It is the day the Holy Spirit descended on the apostles causing them to speak in tongues. (Acts 2:3-4) We as Christians know the Pentecost is important. It represents the beginning of the Christian Church. The disciples saw the crucifixion of Jesus. They saw Him after His resurrection and saw Him ascend to heaven.

Repent and Be Baptized
Acts 2: 37-39

Now when they heard this, they were pricked in their heart and said unto Peter and to the rest of the apostles, "Men and brethren, what shall we do?" Then Peter said to them, "Repent, and be baptized every one of you in the name of Jesus Christ for the remission of sins, and ye shall receive the gift of the Holy Ghost. For the promise is unto you, and to your children, and to all that are afar off, even as many as the Lord our God shall call."

The Spirit Will Be Your Comforter
John 14: 15-17

"If ye love me, keep my commandments. And I will pray to the Father, and He shall give you another Comforter, that He may abide with you forever. Even the Spirit of truth whom the world cannot receive because it seeth Him not, neither knoweth Him, but ye know Him, for He dwelleth with you, and shall be in you."

Leviticus 17: 11

For the life of the flesh is in the blood and I have given it to you upon the altar to make an atonement for your souls for it is the blood that maketh an atonement for the soul.

***Blood is a vital part of life. Without blood, we or any other creature cannot live. Because of this, a blood sacrifice was part of the Jewish people. When blood was shed, it made the people think of life and death. Blood was used on the doorpost at the first Passover. The Jewish law required sacrifice offerings of blood. All this changed after the death of our Lord Jesus Christ.

Hebrews 10: 11-12 And this need changed with the blood shed of Christ.

Chapter 6

Lesson 1
Stephen
Acts 6: 1-7

Stephen was a man chosen to help preach and spread the word. He was a faithful servant of the Lord. He was full of faith and of the Holy Ghost. He was one of the seven men chosen by the Lord to be responsible for the distribution of food to the widows after the apostles saw that they had been ignored and needed help. The other six men are Philip, Prochorus, Nicanor, Timon, Parmenas and Nicolas. The apostles prayed and laid their hands on them. The number of the disciples multiplied.

*** I will only tell of Stephen and his love and loyalty to his Lord Jesus Christ.

Stephen Accused of Blasphemy
Acts 6: 9-15

And Stephen, full of faith and power, did great wonders and miracles among the people. Then there arose certain of the synagogue, which is called the synagogue of the Lobertines, and Cyrenians, and Alexandrians, and of them of Cilicia and of Asia, disputing with Stephen. And they were not able to resist the wisdom and the spirit by which he spake. Then they suborned (bribed) men to say they heard him speak blasphemous words against Moses, and against God. They stirred up the people, the elders, and the scribes, and they came upon him and caught him, and brought him to the council. They set up false witnesses that said he ceaseth not to speak blasphemous words against this holy place, and the law. They said they heard him say, that this Jesus of Nazareth shall destroy this place and change the customs which Moses delivered us. They all sat in the council, looking steadfastly on him and they saw his face as it had been the face of an angel. Stephen was the first person to be stoned to death because of his belief in Jesus Christ.

Stephen Speaks to the Council
Acts 7

Stephen speaks about how the people continued to reject God. He remined them how Abraham, through God led them into the land of Israel and how God made a covenant with him. He told them how Joseph was sold into Egypt: and that God was always with him and how Moses delivered them out of Egypt 400 years later. The people didn't understand. The people said to Aaron, make us gods to go before us: for we don't know what has happened to this Moses which brought us out of Egypt. They made a golden calf and offered sacrifices unto the idol. They didn't realize Moses was with God making the ten commandments. Stephen gave a speech about Jesus and His gospel. The religious leaders falsely accused him of blasphemy. The punishment for blasphemy was death.

Stephen to Accusers
Acts 7: 51-53

Ye stiffnecked and uncircumcised in heart and ears, ye do always resist the Holy Ghost: as your fathers did. Which of the prophets have not your fathers persecuted? And they have slain them which shewed before of the coming of the Just One; of whom ye have been now the betrayers and murderers: who have received the law by the disposition of angels and have not kept it.

Stephen is Stoned
Acts 7: 54-60

When they heard Stephen they were very angry and cut to the heart, and they gnashed or bit on him with their teeth. Stephen was full of the Holy Ghost and he looked into heaven and saw the glory of God, and Jesus standing on the right hand of God. He said, Behold, I see the heavens opened, and the Son of man standing on the right hand of God.
Then they cried with a loud voice, stopped their ears, and ran upon him with one accord. They cast him out of the city and stoned him. <u>The witnesses laid down their clothes at a young man's feet, whose name was Saul.</u> They stoned Stephen calling upon God, and saying, Lord Jesus, receive my spirit. He kneeled down, and cried with a loud voice, Lord, lay not this sin to their charge. And when he had said this, he fell asleep.

Revelation 2: 10

Fear none of those things which thou shalt suffer: behold, the devil shall cast some of you into prison, that ye may be tired; and ye shall have tribulation ten days: be thou faithful unto death, and I will give thee a crown of life.

*** Oh to be like Stephen. He was a faithful servant and preached the gospel boldly of his Lord even unto his own death. We should all strive to read the Bible and learn his word so we can tell others. I want to be a testimony for my Lord in this lost and dying world.

The Church Is Persecuted
Acts 8: 1-3

And Saul was consenting unto his death. And at that time there was a great persecution against the church which was at Jerusalem; and they were all scattered abroad throughout the regions of Judaea and Samaria, except the apostles. Devout men carried Stephen to his burial and made great lamentation over him. They were full of grief and sorrow. As for Saul, he made havoc of the church, entering into every house, and haling men and women and committed them to prison.

Lesson 2

Saul

Saul was from Tarsus and came from a well to do family. He was a young radical in his early life and a man that was a brutal person and always wanted to punish the early church. He was on his way to Damascus to cause more havoc to the church. The Lord struck him blind and he was converted on the road to Damascus. He started preaching and started his missionary journeys. He had been so mean to the Christians, the people still feared him. It took a while before he was trusted. I wonder if the first message Saul truly heard was the preaching of Stephen. Paul became a great preacher for the Lord, he never backed down from preaching the word, even though he was punished many times. He was even stoned and left for dead and he got up and went back into the city he had been preaching in. We will see from some of the following verses, comings and goings and teachings of Paul.

Saul is Blinded For Three Days
Acts 9: 1-9

And Saul, yet breathing out threatenings and slaughter against the disciples of the Lord, went unto the high priest, He desired of him letters to Damascus to the synagogues, that if he found any of this way, whether they were men or women, he might bring them bound unto Jerusalem. And he journeyed, he came near Damascus: and suddenly there shined round about him a light from heaven: and he fell to the earth, and heard a voice saying to him, <u>Saul, Saul, why persecutest thou me?</u> Saul said, Who art thou, Lord? The Lord said, <u>I am Jesus whom thou persecutest: it is hard for thee to kick against the pricks.</u> And he trembling and astonished said, Lord, what wilt thou have me to do? And the Lord said, <u>Arise, and go into the city, and it shall be told thee what thou must do.</u> And the men which journeyed with him stood speechless, hearing a voice, but seeing no man. And Saul arose from the earth; and when his eyes were opened, he saw no man: but they led him by the hand and brought him into Damascus. And he was three days without sight, and neither did eat nor drink.

*** Didn't take Saul long to ask, What wilt thou have me to do? This is when Saul was converted and started working for the LORD!

The Lord Comes to Ananias
Acts 9: 10-18

Ananias, a certain disciple at Damascus, had a vision from the Lord. The Lord told him to, <u>Arise, and go into the street which is called Straight, and enquire in the house of Judas for one called Saul, of Tarsus for, behold, he prayeth, and hath seen in a vision a man name Ananias coming in, and putting his hand on him, that he might receive his sight.</u> Ananias answered, Lord, I have heard from many men, how much evil he hath done to the saints at Jerusalem: he has authority from the chief priest to bind all that call on your name. But the Lord said, <u>Go thy way: for he is a chosen vessel unto me, to bear my name before the Gentiles, and kings, and the children of Israel: For I will shew him how great things he must suffer for my name's sake.</u> Ananias went his way, entered the house; he put his hands on him, and said, Brother Saul, the Lord, Jesus appeared to me and has sent me that you might receive your sight and be filled with the Holy Ghost. And immediately there fell from his eyes as it had been scales: and he received sight and arose and was baptized.

*** So the evil Saul was converted and baptized. (Acts 13: 9) His name was changed to Paul. He started preaching in the synagogues, that Christ is the Son of God. People remembered how he punished others for preaching and some were still afraid of him. Paul became one of the most important people to Jesus and had a great relationship with the Lord. Paul wrote letters to the Romans to prepare the way. He wanted to let them know he is not the person he used to be. He wanted them to know he loves the gospel and Jesus Christ. He told the believing Romans he is an apostle that spreads the teaching of Jesus.

Paul Was Also Stoned
Acts 14: 19

And there came thither certain Jews from Antioch and Iconium, who persuaded the people, and having stoned Paul, drew him out of the city, thinking he was dead. The disciples stood round about him, he got up and came back into the city. The next day he departed with Barnabas to Derbe.

Paul's Journey to Corinth
Acts 18: 1-11

After Paul departed Athens, he came to Corinth. He found a certain Jew named Aquila and his wife Priscilla. Paul stayed with them. He testified to the Jews that Jesus was Christ. And when they opposed themselves, and blasphemed, he shook his raiment, and said to them, Your blood be upon your own heads; I am clean; from henceforth I will go unto the Gentiles. And he departed thence and entered into a certain man's house, named Justus, one that worshipped God, whose house joined hard to the synagogue. And Crispus, the chief ruler of the synagogue, believed on the Lord with all his house; and many of the Corinthians hearing believed, and were baptized. Then spake the Lord to Paul in the night in a vision, <u>Be not afraid, but speak, and hold not thy peace: For I am with thee, and no man shall set on thee to hurt thee: for I have much people in this city.</u> And he continued there a year and six months, teaching the word of God to them.

Priscilla and Aquila

They were husband and wife and Christian workers who moved from place to place to start churches. Paul worked with them and witnessed to the Jews. They worked also as tent makers.

John's Disciples Baptized
Acts 19: 1-6

Paul passed through the upper coast to Ephesus: finding certain disciples, He said to them, Have ye received the Holy Ghost since ye believed? And they said to him, We have not so much as heard whether there be any Holy Ghost. And he said to them, Unto what then were ye baptized? And they said to John's baptism. Paul said, John verily baptized with the baptism of repentance, saying to the people, that they should believe on him which should come after him, that is, on Christ Jesus. When they heard this, they were baptized in the name of the Lord Jesus. And when Paul laid his hands on them, the Holy Ghost came on them; and they spake with tongues and prophesied. And all the men were about twelve.

*** Paul healed many, continued preaching the gospel. He was arrested and bound and put in prison. He preached also to the Gentiles. He urged them to believe in the Lord Jesus Christ and His teachings. He stayed faithful to his Lord.

Paul's Humble Testimony
Acts 22: 1-5

Men, brethren, and fathers, hear ye my defense which I make now unto you. He spoke in Hebrew to them, they kept the more silent: Paul said, I am a Jew, born in Tarsus, a city in Cilicia, yet brought up in this city at the feet of Gamaliel, (Gamaliel was well respected and chosen by God). Paul was taught according to the perfect manner of the law of the fathers, and was zealous toward God, as ye all are this day. I persecuted this way unto the death, binding and delivering into prisons both men and women.

Acts 22: 6-13

As I was on my way to Damascus about noon, suddenly there shone from heaven a great light round about me. I fell to the ground, and heard a voice saying, <u>Saul, Saul, why persecutest thou me?</u> I ask, Who art thou, Lord? He said, <u>I am Jesus of Nazareth, whom thou persecutest.</u> They that were with me saw the light and were afraid; but they heard not the voice of him that spoke to me. I Paul ask Him, Lord, what shall I do? The Lord said, <u>Arise, and go into Damascus; and there it shall be told thee of all things which are appointed for thee to do.</u> And then I could not see, I was led by the ones with me, I came into Damascus. And one Ananias, a devout man according to the law, having a good report of all the Jews which dwelt there, came to me and stood and said to me, Brother Saul, receive thy sight. And the same hour I looked upon him.

Acts 22: 14-21

He told me, The God of our fathers has chosen you, and you should know his will, see that Just One, and should hear the voice of his mouth. You will be his witness to all men of what you have seen and heard. Now why tarry? Arise, be baptized, and wash away thy sins, calling on the name of the Lord. When I came again to Jerusalem, I prayed and was in a trance. And saw him saying unto me, <u>Make haste, and get thee quickly out of Jerusalem: for they will not receive thy testimony concerning me.</u> I said, Lord, they know that I imprisoned and beat in every synagogue them that believed on you, and when the blood of thy martyr Stephen was shed, I also was standing by, and consenting to his death. And the Lord said to me, <u>Depart: for I will send thee far hence unto the Gentiles.</u>

Paul Heading to Rome
Acts 27

Paul was sent to Rome by ship and a storm came and sailing became dangerous. The storm became worse and they lost all hope they could be saved. Paul told them to be of good cheer, no one will be lost among them. For an angel of God stood by me at night, whose I am and whom I serve saying, "Fear not." Paul gave thanks, he encouraged all on the ship. Paul was a prisoner. The ship was lost but all the passengers were saved. Paul's belief in Jesus Christ and God's grace, saved them.

Acts 28: 30-31

Paul dwelt two whole years in his own hired house, and received all that came in to him, Preaching the kingdom of God, and teaching those things which concern the Lord Jesus Christ, with all confidence, no man forbidding him.

Blood of Christ
Romans 5: 1-11

Therefore being justified by faith, we have peace with God through our Lord Jesus Christ: By whom also we have access by faith into this grace wherein stand and rejoice in hope of the glory of God. And not only so, but we glory in tribulations also: knowing that tribulation worketh patience; and patience, experience; and experience, hope: and hope maketh not ashamed; because the love of God is shed abroad in our heart by the Holy Ghost which is given unto us. God when we were yet without strength, in due time Christ died for the ungodly. For scarcely for a righteous man will one die: yet peradventure for a good man some would even dare to die. But God commendeth his love toward us, in that, while we were yet sinners, Christ died for us. Much more the, being now justified by his blood, we shall be saved from wrath through him. For if, when we were enemies, we were reconciled, we shall be saved by his life. And not only so, but we also joy in God through our Lord Jesus Christ, by whom we have now received the atonement.

Newness of Life
Romans 6: 1-4

What shall we say then? Shall we continue in sin, that grace may abound? God forbid. How shall we, that are dead to sin, live any longer therein? Know ye not, that so many of us as were baptized into Jesus Christ were baptized into his death? Therefore we are buried with him by baptism into death: that like as Christ was raised up from the dead by the glory of the Father, even so we also should walk in newness of life.

Higher Power
Romans 13: 1-2

Let every soul be subject unto the higher powers. For there is no power but of God: the powers that be are ordained of God. Whosoever therefore resisteth the power, resisteth the ordinance of God: and they that resist shall receive to themselves damnation.

*** I have tried several times to talk to someone very close to me about salvation and accepting Jesus Christ as their personal Savior. I ask, do you believe in God? He answered with, " I do believe there is a higher power, but I don't know what it is."

Our Body is a Temple
I Corinthians 6: 12-20

All things are lawful unto me, but all things are not expedient: all things are lawful for me, but I will not be brought under the power of any. Meats for the belly, and the belly for meats:

but God shall destroy both it and them, Now the body is not for fornication, but for the Lord; and the Lord for the body. And God hath both raised up the Lord and will also raise up us by his own power. Know ye not that your bodies are the members of Christ? Shall I then take the members of Christ, and make them the members of a harlot? God forbid. What? Know ye not that he which is joined to a harlot is one body? For two, saith he, shall be one flesh. But he that is joined unto the Lord is one spirit. When fornication is committed it is a sin against your own body. What? Know ye not that your body is the temple of the Holy Ghost, which is in you, which ye have of God, and ye are not your own? For ye are bought with a price: therefore glorify God in your body, and in your spirit, which are God's.

The Lord's Supper
I Corinthians 11: 23-27

For I have received of the Lord that which also I delivered unto you, That the Lord Jesus the same night in which also I delivered unto you, That the Lord Jesus the same night in which he was betrayed took bread: And when he had given thanks, he brake it, and said, <u>Take, eat: this is my body, which is broken for you: this do in remembrance of me.</u> After the same manner also he took the cup, when he had supped, saying, <u>this cup is the new testament in my blood: this do ye, as oft as ye drink it in remembrance of me.</u> For as often as ye eat this bread, and drink this cup, ye do shew the Lord's death till he come. Where for whosoever shall eat this bread, and drink this cup of the Lord, unworthily, shall be guilty of the body and blood of the Lord.

*** Examine your heart before you eat the bread and drink the cup.

False Preaching
2 Corinthians 11: 13-15

For such are false apostles, deceitful workers, transforming themselves into the apostles of Christ. And no marvel; for Satan himself is transformed into an angel of light. Therefore it is no great thing if his ministers also be transformed as the ministers of righteousness; whose end shall be according to their works.

Paul's Sufferings
2 Corinthians 11: 23-33

Are they ministers of Christ? (I speak as a fool) I am more; in labors more abundant, in stripes above measure, in prisons more frequent, in deaths oft. Of the Jews five times received I forty stripes save one. Thrice (3) was I beaten with rods, once was I stoned, thrice I suffered shipwreck, a night and a day I have been in the deep. The God and Father of our Lord Jesus Christ, which is blessed for evermore, knoweth that I lie not. In Damascus the governor under Aretas the king kept the city of the Damascenes with a garrison, desirous to apprehend me: And through a window in a basket was I let down by the wall and escaped his hands.

*** Garrison is a body of troops.

The Revelation of Jesus Christ
Galatians 1: 11-18

But I certify you, brethren, that the gospel which was preached of me is not after man. For I neither received it of man, neither was I taught it, but by the revelation of Jesus Christ. For ye have heard of my conversation in time past in the Jews' religion, how that beyond measure I persecuted the church of God and wasted it: and profited in the Jews' religion above many my equals in mine own nation, being more exceedingly zealous of the traditions of my fathers. But when it pleased God, who separated me from my mother's womb, and called me by his grace, To reveal his Son in me, that I might preach him among the heathen; immediately I conferred not with flesh and blood: Neither went I up to Jerusalem to them which were apostles before me; but I went into Arabia and returned again unto Damascus. Then after three years I went up to Jerusalem to see Peter, and abode with him fifteen days.

*** Paul confronts Peter about his hypocrisy. Peter says one thing and does another.

Paul's Charge Against Peter
Galatians 2: 11-16

When Peter came to Antioch, Paul withstood him to the face, because he was to be blamed. For before that certain came from James, he did eat with the Gentiles: but when they were come, he withdrew and separated himself, fearing them which were of the circumcision. And the other Jews dissembled likewise with him; insomuch that Barnabas also was carried away with their dissimulation. But when I saw that they walked not uprightly according to the truth of the gospel, I said unto Peter before them all, if thou, being a Jew, livest after the manner of Gentiles, and not as do the Jews, why compellest the Gentiles to live as do the Jews? We who are Jews by nature, and not sinners of the Gentiles, Knowing that a man is not justified by the works of the law, but by the faith of Jesus Christ, even we have believed in Jesus Christ, that we might be justified by the faith of Christ, and not by the works of the law: for by the works of the law shall no flesh be justified.

*** It doesn't tell in the Bible how Paul died. But, he remained a faithful servant to his Lord Jesus Christ.

Lesson 3

We have studied a small amount about Stephen and Paul. Both men loved the Lord and were dedicated men. They both were treated badly for spreading the gospel about the Lord and salvation. They both wanted to show honor and glory for ever and ever to Jesus Christ. In Lesson 3 we will take a short look at some of the people that traveled with Paul during his ministry.

*** God is a Spirit and He is all around us. He knows our every thought, what we do or say. Are we sure God is satisfied with our behavior??

Barnabas
Acts 4: 36

And Joses, who by the apostles was surnamed Barnabas, (which is, being interpreted, the son of consolation,) a Levite, and of the country of Cyprus.

*** Son of consolation also means encouragement or comfort. Barnabas was not one of the original 12 disciples.

Barnabas and Saul
Acts 9: 26-31

And when Saul was come to Jerusalem, he assayed to join himself to the disciples: but they were all afraid of him, and believed not that he was a disciple. But Barnabas took him, and brought him to the apostles, and declared to them how he had seen the Lord in the way, and he had spoken to him and how he preached boldly at Damascus in the name of Jesus. And he was with them coming in and going out of Jerusalem. And he spake boldly in the name of the Lord Jesus and disputed against the Grecians: but they went about to slay him. Which when the brethren knew, they brought him down to Caesarea, and sent him forth to Tarsus. Then had the churches rest throughout all Judaea and Galilee and Samaria and were edified; and walking in the fear of the Lord, and in the comfort of the Holy Ghost, were multiplied.

Barnabas Goes to Antioch
Acts 11: 19-26

Now they which were scattered abroad upon the persecution that arose about Stephen traveled as far as Phenice, Cyprus, and Antioch, preaching the word to none but to the Jews only. And some of them were men of Cyprus and Cyrene, which, when they came to Antioch, spoke to the Grecians, preaching the Lord Jesus. And the hand of the Lord was with them: and a great number believed and turned to the Lord. Then tidings of these things came unto the ears of the church which was in Jerusalem: and they sent forth Barnabas, that he should go as far as Antioch. Who, when he came, and had seen the grace of God, was glad, and exhorted them all, that with purpose of heart they would cleave unto the LORD. Barnabas was a good man, and full of the Holy Ghost and of faith: and much people was added unto the Lord. Then departed Barnabas to Tarsus, for to seek Saul: when he found him, he brought him to Antioch. And it came to pass, that a whole year they assembled themselves with the church and taught much people. And the disciples were called Christians first in Antioch.

*** <u>Grecian</u> is a Jew by birth.

*** <u>Exhort</u> or encourage or urge someone to do something.

Saul and Barnabas to Cyrus
Acts 13: 1-12

There was in the church that was at Antioch certain prophets and teachers; as Barnabas, and Simeon that was called Niger and Lucius of Cyrene, and Manaen which had been brought up with Herod the tetrarch or ruler, and Saul. As they ministered to the Lord, and fasted, the Holy Ghost said, Separate me Barnabas and Saul for the work I have called them to do. And when they had fasted and prayed, and laid their hands on them, they sent them away. They were sent by the Holy Ghost to Seleucia and they sailed to Cyprus. When they were at Salamis, they preached the word of God in the synagogues of the Jews: and they had also John to their minister. And when they had gone through the isle unto Patmos, they found a certain sorcerer, a false prophet, a Jew, whose name was Bar-jesus: which was with the deputy of the country, Sergius Paulus, a prudent man; who called for Barnabas and Saul, and desired to hear the word of God. But Elymas the sorcerer (for so is his name by interpretation) withstood them, seeking to turn away the deputy from the faith. Then Saul, (who is called Paul,) filled with the Holy Ghost, set his eyes on him, and said, O full of all subtilty and all mischief, thou child of the devil, thou enemy of all righteousness, wilt thou not cease to pervert the right ways of the LORD? And now, behold, the hand of the Lord is upon thee, and thou shalt be blind, not seeing the sun for a season. And immediately there fell on him a mist and a darkness; and he went about seeking some to lead him by the hand. Then the deputy, when he saw what was done, believed, being astonished at the doctrine of the Lord.

<u>Circumcision Disputed</u>
Acts 15: 1-12

And certain men which came down from Judaea taught the brethren, and said, Except ye be circumcised after the manner of Moses, ye cannot be saved. When Paul and Barnabas had no small dissension and disputation with them, they determined that they should go up to Jerusalem unto the apostles and elders about this question. And being brought on their way by the church, they passed through Phenice and Samaria, declaring the conversion of the gentiles: and they caused great joy unto all the brethren. When they got to Jerusalem, they were received of the church, and the apostles and elders, and they declared all things that God had done to them. But there rose up certain of the sect of the Pharisees which believed, saying, That it was needful to circumcise them, and to command them to keep the law of Moses. And the apostles and elders came together for to consider this matter. And when there had been much disputing, Peter rose up, and said to them, Men and brethren, ye know how that a good while ago God made choice among us, that the Gentiles by my mouth should hear the word of the gospel and believe. And God, which knoweth the hearts, bare them witness, giving them the Holy Ghost, even as he did unto us; and put no difference between us and them, purifying their hearts by faith. Now therefore why tempt ye God, to put a yoke upon the neck of the disciples, which neither our fathers nor we were able to bear? But we believe that through the grace of the Lord Jesus Christ we shall be saved, even as they. The multitude kept silent and gave audience to Barnabas and Paul, declaring what miracles and wonders God had wrought among the Gentiles by them.

*** Is it not great to know if we believe that through the grace of the Lord Jesus Christ we shall be saved? We must truly thank God for allowing us Gentiles to be able to truly accept the Lord as our own personal Savior. Praise be to God!!!

Dispute of Paul and Barnabas
Acts 15: 35-41

Paul also and Barnabas continued in Antioch, teaching and preaching the work of the Lord, with many others also. Some days after Paul said to Barnabas, Let us go again and visit our brethren in every city where we have preached the word of the Lord, and see how they do. Barnabas determined to take with them John, whose surname was Mark, But Paul thought not good to take him with them, who departed from them from Pamphylia, and went not with them to the work. The contention was so sharp between them, that they departed asunder one from the other: so Barnabas took Mark, and sailed unto Cyprus; And Paul chose Silas, and departed, being recommended by the brethren unto the grace of God.

Timothy
Acts 16: 1-5

On Paul's second journey with Silas they met a certain disciple named Timotheus, the son of a certain woman, which was Jewess and his father was believed to be a Greek.
This was well reported of by the brethren that were at Lystra and Iconium. Paul had him to go forth with him; Paul took and circumcised him because of the Jews which were in those quarters: for they knew his father was a Greek. As they went through the cities, they delivered them the decrees for them to keep, that were ordained of the apostles and elders which were at Jerusalem. And so were the churches established in the faith and increased in number daily.

Paul's Vision
Acts 16: 6-10

Paul passed through Mysia and came down to Troas. And a vision appeared to Paul in the night; There stood a man of Macedonia, and prayed him, saying, Come over into Macedonia, and help us. And after he had seen the vision, immediately we endeavored to go into Macedonia, assuredly gathering that the Lord had called us for to preach the gospel unto them.

Lydia
Acts 16: 12-19

They came to Philippi, which is the chief city of that part of Macedonia, and a colony: and we were in that city abiding certain days. And on the sabbath we went out of the city by a river side, where prayer was wont to be made; we sat down and spoke to the women which resorted thither. A certain woman named Lydia, a seller of purple, of the city of Thyatira, which worshiped God, heard us: whose heart the Lord opened, that she attended unto the things which were spoken of Paul. And when she was baptized, and her household, she besought us, saying, If ye have judged me to be faithful to the Lord, come into my house, and abide there. And she constrained (compelled) us. And it came to pass, as we went to prayer, a certain damsel possessed with a spirit of divination (attempting to foretell the future) met us, which brought her masters much gain by soothsaying (prediction or art of foretelling events): The same followed Paul and us, and cried, saying, These men are the servants of the most high God, which shew unto us the way of salvation. And this did she many days. But Paul, being grieved, turned and said to the spirit, I command thee in the name of Jesus Christ to come out of her. And he came out the same hour. And when her masters saw that the hope of their gains was gone, they caught Paul and Silas, and drew them into the marketplace unto the rulers.

Paul and Silas
Acts 16: 20-25

The masters brought them to the magistrates, saying, these men, being Jews, do exceeding trouble our city. They teach customs, which are not lawful for us to receive, neither to observe, being Romans. And the multitude rose up together against them: and the magistrates rent off their clothes and commanded to beat them. Then they put them in prison, charging the jailor to keep them safely: who, having received such a charge, trust them into the inner prison, and made their feet fast in the stocks. And at midnight Paul and Silas prayed and sang praises unto God: and the prisoners heard them.

Prison Keepers Converted
Acts 16: 26-40

Suddenly there was a great earthquake, the foundations of the prison were shaken: immediately all the doors were opened and every one's bands were loosed. The keeper of the prison woke up, saw the prison doors open and drew out his sword to kill himself because he thought all the prisoners had fled. Paul cried in a loud voice, Do not harm yourself, for we are all here. Then he called for a light and came trembling and fell down before Paul and Silas. He ask them, what must I do to be saved? They said, Believe on the Lord Jesus Christ, and you shall be saved and thy house. He took them the same hour of the night and washed their stripes; and was baptized, he and all his, straightway. When he brought them to his house, he set meat before them, they rejoiced, believing in God with all his house. When it was day, the magistrates sent the serjeants, saying, Let those men go. The keeper of the prison told Paul and he said to them, They have beaten us openly uncondemned, being Romans, and have cast us into prison; and now do they thrust us out privily? Nay verily; but let them come and fetch us out. The serjeants told the magistrates: and they feared when they heard that they were Romans. And they came and besought them, and brought them out, and desired them to depart out of the city. They went out of the prison and entered into the house of Lydia: and when they had seen the brethren, they comforted them and departed.

Timothy

Paul loved Timothy and knew he was a servant of God. I Thessalonians 3:2, Paul describes Timothy as, our brother, and minister of God, and our fellow laborer in the gospel of Christ, to establish you, and to comfort you concerning your faith.

Paul Speaking to Timothy
1 Timothy 1: 1-3

Paul, an apostle of Jesus Christ by the commandment of God our Savior, and Lord Jesus Christ, which is our hope; Unto Timothy, my own son in the faith; grace, mercy and peace, from God our Father and Jesus Christ our Lord. Paul left Timothy at Ephesus, when I went into Macedonia, that thou mightest charge some that they teach no other doctrine. To be true and faithful to the Lord Jesus Christ.

Paul Speaking About Timothy
2 Timothy 1: 1-7

Paul said, my dearly beloved son: Grace, mercy and peace, from God the Father and Christ Jesus our Lord. I thank God, whom I serve from my forefather with pure conscience, that without ceasing I have remembrance of thee in my prayers night and day. He speaks about his unfeigned (sincere or genuine) faith, that dwelt first in his grandmother Lois, and his mother Eunice. Paul wanted to stir up the gift of God, which is in Timothy by putting on of his hands. For God hath not given us the spirit of fear; but of power, and love and of a sound mind.

God's Mercy Toward Paul
I Timothy 1:12-17

And I thank Christ Jesus our Lord, who hath enabled me, for that he counted me faithful, putting me into ministry; who was before a blasphemer, a persecutor, and injurious: but I obtained mercy, because I did it ignorantly in unbelief. And the grace of our Lord was exceeding abundant with faith and love which is in Christ Jesus. This is a faithful saying, and worthy of all acceptation, that Christ Jesus came into the world to save sinners; of whom I am chief. Howbeit for this cause I obtained mercy, that in me first, Jesus Christ might shew forth all long suffering, for a pattern to them which should here after believe on him to life everlasting. Now unto the King eternal, immortal, invisible, the only wise God, be honor and glory for ever and ever, Amen.

*** He wanted to show honor and glory for ever and ever to Jesus Christ.

Root of All Evil
1 Timothy 6: 6-10

But godliness with contentment is great gain. For we brought nothing into this world, and it is certain we can carry nothing out. And having food and raiment let us be therewith content. But they that will be rich fall into temptation and a snare, and into many foolish and hurtful lusts, which drown men in destruction and perdition (destruction or ruin). For the love of money is the root of all evil; which while some coveted after, they have erred from the faith, and pierced themselves through with many sorrows.

Testimony of The Lord
2 Timothy 1: 8-12

Be not thou therefore ashamed of the testimony of our Lord, not of me his prisoner: but be thou partaker of the afflictions of the gospel according to the power of God; Who hath saved us, and called us with an holy calling, not according to our works, but according to his own purpose and grace, which was given us in Christ Jesus before the world began, But is now made manifest by the appearing of our Savior Jesus Christ, who hath abolished death, and hath brought life and immortality to light through the gospel: Whereunto I am appointed a preacher, an apostle, and a teacher of the Gentiles. For the which cause I also suffer these things: never the less I am not ashamed: for I know whom I have believed and am persuaded that he is able to keep that which I have committed unto him against that day.

Preach God's Word
2 Timothy 4: 2-7

Preach the word; be instant in season, out of season: reprove, rebuke, exhort with all longsuffering and doctrine. For the time will come when they will not endure sound doctrine; but after their own lusts shall they heap to themselves teachers, having itching ears; and they shall turn away their ears from the truth, and shall be turned unto fables. But watch thou in all things, endure afflictions, do the work of an evangelist, make full proof of thy ministry. For I am now ready to be offered, and the time of my departure is at hand. I have fought a good fight, I have finished my course, I have kept the faith. Henceforth there is laid up for me a crown of righteousness, which the Lord, the righteous judge, shall give me at that day:

and not to me only, but unto all them also that love his appearing.

*** This makes me think of people I have spoken to about salvation and doing wrong. They don't want to endure sound doctrine. They feel they have all the answers to continue how they are living. We must continue to teach the word and we may endure suffering. We must fulfill the ministry God has given us to do.

Titus

Titus was a faithful trusted servant of the Lord. He traveled with Paul and Barnabas. Titus was a born again Gentile. Titus and Timothy both helped Paul.

Titus 2: 1-2

Paul wrote from Corinth when he was released from prison. Teach sound doctrine, the aged men and women also to be sober, grave, temperate, sound in faith, charity, and in patience. Paul told them how to minister to all. He closed his letter with all that are with me salute thee. Greet them that love us in faith. Grace be with you all. Amen.

*** Paul tells Titus to choose good leaders

Qualifications for Leaders
Titus 1:5-9

For this cause left I thee in Crete, that thou shouldest set in order the things that are wanting, and ordain elders in every city, as I had appointed thee: If any be blameless, the husband of one wife, having faithful children not accused of riot or unruly. For a bishop must be blameless, as the steward of God; not self-willed, not soon to angry, not given to wine, no striker, not given to filthy lucre (a monetary gain or reward); But a lover of hospitality, a lover of good men, sober, just, holy, temperate; Holding fast the faithful word as he hath been taught, that he may be able by sound doctrine both to exhort and to convince the gainsayers (to deny, dispute, or contradict, to speak or act against; oppose).

*** If you are saved and a believer of Christ, your actions better back you up. Can the Lord depend on you or I to sail by faith when we face the storms? Let's always remember that God's spirit is all around us. Are we sure He is satisfied with our behavior?

Lesson 4

In Lesson 3, we read a little about a few people associated with Paul. Barnabas, Timothy, Silas, Titus, and a lady named Lydia. Paul was very faithful to his Lord and Savior Jesus Christ. I think of my friend Rae sometimes when I think of Paul. He was a sinner and the Lord saved him. And he became a man on fire for the Lord. Rae was a sinner saved by grace and she is SO on fire for her Lord! Oh, to be like them! In this lesson, we will touch on works and faith from the book of James. My favorite verse is Hebrews 11: 1. Now faith is the substance of things hoped for, the evidence of things not seen. I was worried one time about my health and I just knew I had lung cancer. I had a "spot" on my left lung and I hurt a lot. A PET scan was ordered. I was told this scan will show everything from your eyes to your thighs. Prayer warriors were praying for me. The day I had the scan, I was reading my verse and the next verse reads: For by it the elders obtained a good report. When I read this, there was a calm that came over me. The Lord showed me through His word that I was going to be okay.

*** No one knows for sure who wrote the book of James. Jesus had a half-brother named James and he may be the author. James grew up as Jesus did with Mary and Joseph in Nazareth. He didn't believe Jesus was Lord until the end of Jesus' earthly ministry. James was a leader of the Jerusalem church.

The Tribes Greeted
James 1: 1

James, a servant of God and of the Lord Jesus Christ, to the twelve tribes which are scattered abroad, greeting.

***The 12 tribes which are scattered abroad refers to Christians who were by persecution driven out and scattered from Jerusalem.

*** Since James was the leader of the Jerusalem congregation, It was only natural he write to them regarding their faith.

*** He reminded them that God had accepted the Gentiles by faith alone and not on Jewish terms. Peter emphasized that it was God's choice to give the gospel to the Gentiles and that He who directed this mission had given them the Holy Ghost, even as He had done unto the Jewish believers. Each speaker in this conference made it clear that salvation is by faith alone.

*** We must truly thank God for allowing us Gentiles,
 to be able to accept the Lord as our own personal Savior.

Trials, Temptations and Wisdom
James 1: 2-16

James speaks of asking God for wisdom, that giveth to all men liberally, upbraideth not; and it shall be given. Ask in faith, nothing wavering. For he that wavereth is like a wave of the sea driven with the wind and tossed. Verse 12-15: Blessed is the man that endureth temptation: for when he is tried, he shall receive the crown of life, which the Lord hath promised to them that love him. Let no man say when he is tempted, I am tempted of God: for God cannot be tempted with evil, neither tempteth he any man: But everyman is tempted, when he is drawn away of his own lust, and enticed. Then when lust hath conceived, it bringeth forth sin: and sin, when it is finished, bringeth forth death. Do not err, my beloved brethren.

James 1: 22-23

But be ye doers of the word, and not hearers only, deceiving your own selves. For if any be a hearer of the word, and not a doer, he is like unto a man beholding his natural face in a glass.

*** When we read and study the Bible we plant a seed in our heart. We end up with spiritual growth or fruit. God is so good to us. When we are tempted, if our heart has that seed planted, then our heart belongs to God. We can and will have the strength to say **NO** to our temptations.

Don't Show Favoritism
James 2: 1-5

My brethren, have not the faith of our Lord Jesus Christ, the LORD of glory, with respect of persons. For if there come unto your assembly a man with a gold ring, in goodly apparel, and there come in also a poor man in vile raiment; And ye have respect to him that weareth the gay clothing, and say unto him, Sit thou here in a good place; and say to the poor, Stand thou there, or sit here under my footstool: Are ye not then partial in yourselves, and are become judges of evil thoughts?

Hearken, my beloved brethren, Hath not God chosen the poor of this world rich in faith, and heirs of the kingdom which he hath promised to them that love him?

*** Have you ever been guilty of this? I'm sure I have and I am very ashamed of it. When I read this, I remembered a story I read once, about a preacher that dressed like a homeless man, dirty clothes, hair a mess. He was sitting on the steps of his church and when the congregation came in, most of them completely ignored him. Some walked, so as not to get close to him. When the preacher revealed himself to his flock, they of course were very ashamed. Who are we to judge?

Hebrews 13: 1-2

Let brotherly love continue. Be not forgetful to entertain strangers: for thereby some have entertained angels unawares.

Faith and Works Go Together
James 2: 14-20

What doth it profit, my brethren, though a man say he hath faith, and have not works? Can faith save him? If a brother or sister be naked, and destitute of daily food, And one of you say unto them, Depart in peace, be ye warmed and filled; notwithstanding ye give them not those things which are needful to the body; what doth it profit? Even so faith, if it hath not works, is dead, being alone. Yes, a man may say, Thou hast faith, and I have works: shew me thy faith without thy works, and I will shew thee my faith by my works. Thou believest that there is one God; thou doest well; the devils also believe, and tremble. But wilt thou know, O vain man, that faith without works is dead?"

Isaiah 64:6

But we are all as an unclean thing, and all our righteousnesses are as filthy rags; and we all do fade as a leaf; and our iniquities, like the wind, have taken us away.

*** No matter the good we do – it cannot save us. Only and through the blood of the Lord Jesus Christ.

*** I personally believe if we are saved we will do works, with faith for our Lord. We will be good people, we will want to see all our family and friends saved. Even our enemies. We should pray for all. Work- believing and have faith.

Galatians 2:16

Knowing that a man is not justified by the works of the law, but by the faith of Jesus Christ, even we have <u>believed</u> in Jesus Christ, that we might be <u>justified</u> by the faith of Christ, and not by the works of the law: for by the works of the law shall no flesh be <u>justified</u>.

That Old Tongue
James 3: 8

But the tongue can no man tame; it is an unruly evil, full of deadly poison.

*** There are times when we say things that may not be really true or we may "stretch" the truth. Then we regret the words that may hurt someone. There may be words said that can cause a long friendship to end.

*** My sweet momma kept a little magnet on her refrigerator with these words. "Lord, keep your arm around my shoulder and your hand over my mouth."

James 4: 1-12

God wants us to draw near to Him. He said, whosoever therefore will be a friend of the world is the enemy of God. Do ye think that the scripture saith in vain, The spirit that dwelleth in us lusteth to envy? But he giveth more grace. Wherefore he saith, God resisteth the proud, but giveth grace to the humble. Submit yourselves therefore to God. Resist the devil, and he will flee from you. He doesn't want us speaking evil of another. He that speaketh evil of his brother, and judgeth his brother, speaketh evil of the law, and judgeth the law.

Be Careful When Boasting
James 4: 13-17

Go to now, ye that say, today or tomorrow we will go into such a city, and continue there a year, and buy and sell, and get gain. Whereas ye know not what shall be on the morrow. For what is your life? It is even a vapor, that appeareth for a little time, and then vanisheth away. For ye ought to say, If the Lord will, we shall live, and do this, or that. But not ye rejoice in your boastings: all such rejoicing is evil. Therefore to him that knoweth to do good, and doeth it not, to him it is sin.

James 5:16

Confess your faults one to another, and pray one for another, that ye may be healed. The effectual fervent prayer of a righteous man availeth much.

Hebrews 3:3-4

For this man was counted worthy of more glory than Moses, inasmuch as he who hath builded the house. hath more honor than the house. For every house is builded by some man; but he that built all things is God.

Hebrews 8:1

Now of the things which we have spoken, this is the sum: We have such a High Priest, who is set on the right hand of the throne of the Majesty in the heavens.

*** Jesus is the High Priest. He has His ministry in heaven and sits on the right hand of God.

<u>Hebrews 12: 28-29</u>

Wherefore we receiving a kingdom which cannot be moved, let us have grace, whereby we may serve God acceptably with reverence and godly fear: for our God is a consuming fire.

*** We must serve God with grace, reverence, and godly fear. When we go to God's house, we must always show reverence. I feel we should dress our best, appropriately for our Lord when we go to His house. Enter to worship Him with love and godly fear.

*** Peter spoke about scoffers (a person who mocks or makes fun of someone or something, often of religion or moral values) coming in the last days. They will make fun of our beliefs. Peter told them to be mindful of the words spoken by the holy prophets. Judgement will come to these ungodly men. They felt they can live however they wish. The world was overflowed and destroyed by water and perished. The heaven and earth which are now by the same word are reserved unto fire against the day of judgement and perdition (loss of the soul) of ungodly men.

<u>Jude</u>

Jude refers himself as the brother of James. There is more than one James in the Bible and he could possibly be talking about James the half-brother of Jesus, so Jude may also be half-brother to Jesus. He spoke of ungodly men turning the grace of God into lasciviousness and denying the only LORD God and our Lord Jesus Christ. Jude confronted these sinful teachers. Jude taught and encouraged godly living and to stand firm in our faith.

*** <u>Lasciviousness</u> – Sexual behavior or conduct that is considered crude and offensive or contrary to moral or other standards of appropriate behavior. Unrestrained sexual behavior. Lustfulness.

Lesson 5

As we finish up our study. I hope we will continue to study His word and grow. In the end of our journey here on earth, the things we have, are, just that, things. The most important thing is to know that, The Lord Jesus Christ is our own personal Savior.
<u>NOTHING ELSE MATTERS!</u>

<u>1 John</u>

Speaks of walking in the light and we are to confess our sins. God is light and in him is no darkness at all. If we say we have fellowship with him, and walk in darkness, we lie, and do not the truth: But if we walk in the light, as he is in the light, we have fellowship one with another, and the blood of Jesus Christ his Son cleanseth us from all sin. This is His commandment, that we should believe on the name of his Son Jesus Christ and love one another. Abide in Him. Love your brother, love not the world. Do not deny that Jesus is the Christ. Anyone who denieth the Lord Jesus Christ is an Antichrist.

2 John 1: 1-4

The elder unto the elect lady and her children, whom I love in the truth; and not I only, but also all they that have known the truth. For the truth's sake, which dwelleth in us, and shall be with us forever. Grace be with you, mercy, and peace, from God the Father, and from the Lord Jesus Christ, the Son of the Father, in truth and love. I rejoiced greatly and I found thy children walking in truth, as we have received a commandment from the Father.

*** John was referring to the elder elect lady and her children. She was a godly woman of truth and she taught her children also to be godly and walk in truth. He rejoiced greatly for them and their faithfulness.

2 John 1: 5-8

And now I beseech thee, lady, not as though I wrote a new commandment unto thee, but that which we had from the beginning, that we love one another. And this is love that we walk after his commandments. This is the commandment, that as ye have heard from the beginning, ye should walk in it. There are many deceivers entered into the world, who confess not that Jesus Christ is come in the flesh. This is a deceiver and an antichrist. Look to yourselves, that we lose not those things which we have wrought, but that we receive a full reward.

The Doctrine of Christ
2 John 1: 9-13

Whosoever transgresseth, and abideth not in the doctrine of Christ, hath not God. He that abideth in the doctrine of Christ, he hath both the Father and the Son. If there come any unto you, and bring not this doctrine, receive him not into your house, neither bid him God speed: If you bid him God speed then you are a partaker of his evil deeds. Having many things to write unto you, I would not write with paper and ink: but I trust to come unto you, and speak face to face, that our joy may be full. The children of the elect sister greet thee. Amen.

3 John

Third John was written to Gaius, a faithful member of the church whom John praised for showing unselfish devotion to the cause of Christ by providing accommodations for God's traveling servants.

John The Apostle

John was one of the 12 apostles. He was at the foot of the cross and witnessed the crucifixion of the LORD. John 19: 26-27 - When Jesus saw His mother and John, His beloved disciple, standing by, Jesus saith unto His mother, woman, behold thy son." Then saith to the disciple, "Behold thy mother." And from that hour, that disciple, John, took her into his own home. John was exiled to an isle called Patmos because of his work of God and for the testimony of Jesus Christ. God gave John visions of the final days on earth. John outlived the other apostles. It is believed he died of natural causes.

***John through his visions saw that the devil and his followers will be judged and that Jesus will overcome or defeat the devil forever. The Lord Jesus will come back for us, His people who are believers. He will be our King forever and take His place on the throne. John said, Revelation 21: 1-2 - And I saw a new heaven, and a new earth: for the first heaven and the first earth were passed away; and there was no more sea. And I John saw the holy city, New Jerusalem, coming down from God out of heaven, prepared as a bride adorned for her husband.

Jesus, The Bright and Morning Star
Revelation 22: 12-13

And, behold, I come quickly; and my reward is with me, to give every man according as his work shall be. I am Alpha and Omega, the beginning and the end, the first and the last.

The Book of Revelation Ends
Revelation 22: 20-21

He which testifieth these things saith, Surely I come quickly. Amen. Even so, come, Lord Jesus. The grace of our Lord Jesus Christ be with you all. Amen.

Linda Sue Hand Hayes

About the Author

Linda Hand Hayes resides in Abingdon, Virginia, with her husband Jerry. She has two sons, Chad and Aaron McGlamery; five precious grandchildren: Joseph, Zackery, Maci, Landen, and Amelia; and several step grandchildren with two, Edith and Wyatt, that call her Nanna Linda. She also had an exchange student named Philip that is married to Mendy and they have a son, Nathan. They live in Los Angeles, California. Philip still calls her "Mom."

I had always told the Lord, "I will sing or play the piano, and go to Bible Studies. But Lord, don't ever expect me to lead a Bible Study. I can't. I won't. One day, my friend Rae asked me if I would meet with her and study the Bible. I thought about what I had told the Lord, and I said, "SURE!" I told a friend about it, and she said, "Oh, I would love to meet with you, also." Knowing Rae is starving for the Word and stories from the Bible, I thought, *If I am going to help her, I need to do some heavy studying myself.* So, I started reading the Bible and studying more. I could feel the Holy Spirit as I studied. I had such a wonderful time just feeling the presence of the Lord with me. I finally finished all I had written and by now more people wanted to join the study. Well, I learned one thing, you don't ever tell God you are not going to do something. We started our first Bible Study with six wonderful ladies, and you guessed it, I am leading my first Bible Study. Let's remember where we came from, where we have been, where we are, and most of all, where we are going.

www.ingramcontent.com/pod-product-compliance
Lightning Source LLC
Chambersburg PA
CBHW080239170426
43192CB00014BA/2499